l who received a Nobel Prize as did **Trudy Elion** who also struggled to find
female rabbi until they learned about **Regina Jonas** who was portrayed by
sador just like **David Saperstein** who worked with **Lynne Landsberg** in a
as did **Bob Dylan** who got his musical start at a Jewish summer camp like
bert Bourla who led the development of a revolutionary vaccine like **Jonas**
hlo, who learned to draw while recovering in bed as did **Maurice Sendak**
omic that memorialized **Judith Resnik** who before becoming an astronaut
ow who protested the Vietnam War like **Bella Abzug** who served in Congress
o fought f ... who
Gershom ... like
itz who w ... **gnes**
ekutieli ... g to
nnie Leib ... sted
st like **Cla** ... l the
o was play ... like
March for ... **berg**
lped prese ... d by
on Big Ban ... ding
graduate ... nt in
y Koufax ... **andi**
on Capito ... firm
reme Cour ... like
ied archite ... itect
is designs ... him
mmunity ... like
ichael Twi ... was
to himsel ... does
d by **Imi L** ... the
heryl San ... nent
o is a Gra ... olice
to Argent ... left

This Book Belongs To:

Rabin who believed in the Israeli peace movement like **Edward Kessler** who
ng like **Isaac Mizrachi** who built a business empire from nothing like **Jennie**
us basketball championships as did **Sue Bird** who advocates for pay equity
d wanted to help as did **Danny Siegel** who studied at the Jewish Theological
ike **Abby Stein** who stands up for transgender rights and inclusion as does
owe who needed to advocate for herself in school as did **Alma Hernandez**
out relationships and identity as did **Ann Landers** and **Abigail Van Buren**
who did research into the space sciences as did **Arno Penzias** who escaped
ouza who is a self-taught artist like **Mel Blanc** who said, "That's All Folks!"

Heroes With Chutzpah

101 True Tales of Jewish Trailblazers, Changemakers & Rebels

Kerry Olitzky & Deborah Bodin Cohen
Author — Author & Illustrator

Ben Yehuda Press
Teaneck, New Jersey

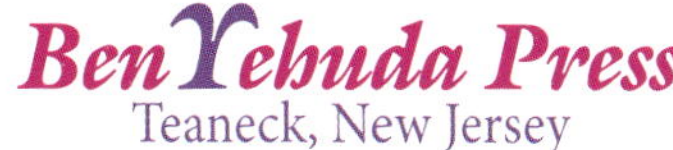

Published by Ben Yehuda Press
122 Ayers Court #1B
Teaneck, NJ 07666
http://www.BenYehudaPress.com

To subscribe to our monthly book club and support independent Jewish publishing, visit https://www.patreon.com/BenYehudaPress.

Ben Yehuda Press books may be purchased at a discount by synagogues, book clubs, and other institutions buying in bulk.
For information, please email markets@BenYehudaPress.com.

For photo credits, see page 210 which constitutes an extension of this copyright page.

Visit **www.heroeswithchutzpah.com** for sources used in this book and updates on related projects.

ISBN13 978-1-953829-61-0

23 24 25 / 10 9 8 7 6 5 4 3 2 1 20231031

Printed in the USA
Signature Book Printing, www.sbpbooks.com

Dedication

For Jerome Reznick, of blessed memory
—KO

For Arianna, Jesse, and Ezra
—DBC

Contents

"Knowledge is limited.
Imagination encircles the world."
Albert Einstein

Dear Reader,

In this book, you will meet 101 Jewish heroes from the last 125 years—scientists and statesmen, artists and athletes, inventors and activists whose impact has been felt around the globe. Their accomplishments are as diverse as their backgrounds. But each one, in their own way, did something worthwhile to make the world a better place.

What makes a hero? We struggled with this question. Heroes have persistence, courage, creativity, and resolve. Albert Einstein, who was born a little too early to be included in this book, was a hero not because of his brilliance, but because he used his talents for good and saw himself as a changemaker.

Chutzpah is a Yiddish word meaning persistence and grit. More than talent or intelligence, heroism requires hard work, dedication, and sacrifice.

Want to know a secret? You can be a hero, too. As you read through this book, think about your talents, convictions, and dreams for the future. What will you do to make the world a better place? What worthwhile thing do you aspire to do? You will meet 101 heroes in this book. You already know the next potential hero—it's you. At the end of the book, you will find blank pages for you to fill out about one of your heroes.

We learned so much when researching and writing this book. We chose 101 heroes but easily could have selected many, many more. May this book inspire you to recognize the heroes in your life and the heroism within you.

Happy reading!

Kerry & Debbie

Sarah Silverman

Outspoken Actor & Comedian, 1970–

When she was young, Sarah's father taught her swear words for fun and then loved to laugh at her bad language. At the same time, Sarah's mother had a classic theater background and wanted Sarah to use clear, polite language. Both of Sarah's parents had a strong influence on her.

Growing up in a small New Hampshire town with few Jewish people, Sarah often felt like an outsider. As she puts it, she was a small person with big teeth. So, she used jokes to get attention and make friends. "I became a comedian because I needed to be funny to be liked," says Sarah. She has gone on to perform on *Saturday Night Live*, *Comedy Central*, her own podcasts, and in movies like *Wreck it Ralph*, *The Aristocrats*, and *School of Rock*.

Sarah liked being with people when she was a kid but pulled back from her friends as a teenager, struggling with depression. Her friendships were suddenly more work than fun. She remembers sobbing, describing her depression as feeling "like I'm desperately homesick, but I'm home." While therapy and medication help, Sarah still suffers from depressive episodes. Sarah says her comedy is the best way for her to cope. She uses her vulnerability to help her become a better comic.

In her comedy routines, Sarah talks about other serious things, like racism, homophobia, sexism, antisemitism, politics, and religion. She likes to joke about taboo topics to make them feel a little less taboo. Besides, whenever somebody tells her not to say something, Sarah feels more like she has to say it. "I believe being a comedian is about exposing yourself, warts and all," says Sarah.

Sarah's sister Susan is a rabbi, but Sarah considers herself a secular Jew. "I talk about being Jewish a lot," says Sarah. "It's funny because I do think of myself as Jewish ethnically, but I'm not religious at all. I have no religion."

Sarah likes to keep an open mind, both onstage and offstage. She listens to everybody, even people she disagrees with, and tries to find common ground. She says, "Stop rolling your eyes and be our allies. We all need each other."

Sarah Silverman's brother-in-law is . . .

TONIGHT!

Yossi Abramowitz

Solar Farmer known as "Captain Sunshine," 1964–

Yossi has been an activist since he was young. His mother would pull him from class at his Jewish day school in Boston to attend workshops about civil disobedience. As he put it, "By 8th grade, I was literate Jewishly and unafraid of police attack dogs and tear gas."

As a college student at Boston University, Yossi supported causes like racial equality for Blacks in South Africa and freedom of religion for Jews in Russia, Ukraine, and other Soviet-controlled areas. He designed his own major: Jewish Public Policy. When the university told Yossi that he couldn't hang an anti-apartheid flag out his dorm window, Yossi fought back. He sued the school and won, paving the way for greater free speech on college campuses.

After college, Yossi earned a graduate degree in journalism. Then he and his wife, Rabbi Susan Silverman, started a family. They have five children, two of whom they adopted from Ethiopia. In 2006, the family moved to Israel. When they got to their new home at Kibbutz Ketura in the Negev Desert, Yossi was stunned that people weren't using solar power in the super sunny region. He decided to change that. First, he set up a solar field at Kibbutz Ketura. Then he set up more solar fields in the Arava Desert. Now, the whole area between the Red Sea and Dead Sea in Israel gets all its power from the sun. Yossi says his environmentalism is a form of Zionism.

Yossi co-founded the Arava Power Company, which focuses on solar energy in Israel. He also co-founded Energiya Global, which helps other countries to start using solar power, especially countries in Africa. Energiya Global has built solar fields in over a dozen countries. "To realize that the same sun shines equally on all of us, is owned by none of us, and can supply our energy needs in abundance, inherently promotes peace. The sun doesn't recognize borders," says Yossi.

Today, Yossi is called Israel's "Captain Sunshine." CNN has called him one of the six leading "green pioneers" on the planet. Yossi is an environmentalist, entrepreneur, four-time nominee for the Nobel Peace Prize and, more than anything else, an optimist. Yossi's advice? "Values are what you live by, vision is what you live towards, and leadership is just simply living your values towards your vision. So, anyone can do it. Anyone can be a leader."

One of Yossi Abramowitz's professors was . . .

Elie Wiesel

Witness, Writer & Activist for Tolerance, 1928–2016

Elie loved words. Words filled his universe in his Romanian childhood home. His mother encouraged his love of Jewish texts. His father fostered his love of modern literature. But then the Nazis came with words of hate. They spoke of ridding the world of Jews. The Nazis acted on their words, deporting Jews like Elie, his parents and baby sister to concentration camps. The Nazis' words fueled the Holocaust, the systematic murder of six million Jews.

Elie survived two concentration camps: Auschwitz and Buchenwald. After the Holocaust, he didn't talk about the horrors he saw in the camps. He didn't know if he had the words to describe what he endured. Elie did not talk about the long ride in packed cattle cars to Auschwitz, or arriving and seeing his mother and sister for the last time before they were killed. He did not talk about being forced to do hard labor next to his father and certainly not about his father's death. But Elie could never forget what he saw. He remembered every detail, every experience.

Elie was a teenager when World War II ended. He was sent to an orphanage in France. A new word described him: survivor. He went to college and found work as a journalist. Reporting for an Israeli newspaper, Elie interviewed the novelist François Mauriac, who talked about the war and seeing Jewish children put in cattle cars to be deported. Elie shared that he had been one of those children. Deeply moved, François convinced Elie to write his story down and bear witness to the atrocities. Once Elie started to write, he couldn't stop. The words flowed out of him. He wrote a 900-page manuscript in Yiddish. He shortened it into a book in French entitled *La Nuit* or *Night*. Translated into over 30 languages, *Night* sold over seven million copies. After *Night*, Elie wrote 50 other books, including *Dawn*, *Day*, and *The Trial of God*. For many people, Elie Wiesel's words became *the* witness of the horrors of the Holocaust.

Elie transformed his pain from the Holocaust into action. He became a fierce advocate for human rights, speaking out for Soviet Jews, Bosnian genocide victims, Cambodian refugees, and many others.

Elie knew over a half dozen languages. He thought in Yiddish, wrote in French, and spoke in English. No matter the language, his message was clear: "The opposite of love is not hate, it's indifference."

Elie Wiesel received a Nobel Prize. So did . . .

human
dignity is
become
ever men
are persecuted
or political views that
at that
the center of
a life even
deep
Love
obsession,
but sharing.
superior;
faith is
wrong. Only
acists
The opposite
not hate,
indiffe
is not
it's
The opposite of
heresy
indiffe
of life is not
it's
Think higher,
human being
times when we are
werle
revent injustice,
be a tim
One person of
integrity
a difference.
a person
esn't have
missing in his or
er humanity
erson can almost be
ined by his or her
very close to
to the French
m, which
casionally
places.
therefore,
my books have been
itten in Fr
Huma
men and
men
e. Jewish history is
of sufferi
and terri
full of
le joy. We
the suffering
remembra
For us
option. No one
as capable
gratitude as one who
has emerged from the

Gertrude "Trudy" Elion

Pioneering Female Scientist, 1918–1999

Trudy graduated from her Bronx, New York, high school when she was just 15. "I think perhaps it was my mother who influenced me the most. She was a housewife. She had no higher education but had the most common sense of anyone I knew, and she wanted me to have a career," explained Trudy.

Trudy's grandfather had arrived from Russia when she was three. Trudy loved him dearly. The same year she graduated high school, her grandfather died of stomach cancer. Watching him suffer influenced her life's path and her decision about what to study in college. She decided to study chemistry in the hope of finding a cure for cancer. "I was highly motivated to do something that might eventually lead to a cure for this terrible disease," shared Trudy.

She graduated college during the Great Depression of the 1930s. Jobs were hard to find, especially for women. "I hadn't been aware that any doors were closed to me until I started knocking on them," Trudy said. She found a temporary position teaching biochemistry to nursing students and an unpaid internship with a chemist. Finally, she saved enough money for graduate school at New York University.

During World War II, more laboratory jobs became available to women as many men left to fight. Trudy found a position, working with scientist George Hitchings. They became research partners for decades. "I never felt constrained to remain strictly in chemistry, but was able to broaden my horizons into biochemistry, pharmacology, immunology, and eventually virology. Each series of studies was like a mystery story," remarked Trudy.

When Trudy was 32, she made her first major discovery: a medicine that fought childhood leukemia. When the drug worked, Trudy was elated. "Our feeling of reward was immeasurable," said Trudy. She went on to develop many other drugs for cancer and other diseases. By the end of her career, Trudy held 45 patents for medicines that she developed.

For her contributions, Trudy, Hitchings, and another scientist shared a Nobel Prize in Medicine in 1988. They received the Nobel Prize not for one specific drug, but for pioneering a rational, scientific approach to drug development that scientists still use today. "Science to me is almost like a religion. To me, science is truth and truth is beautiful," said Trudy.

Trudy Elion struggled to find work because of her gender.
So did . . .

FOR
DISCOVERIES
OF
PRINCIPLES
FOR
DRUG
TREATMENT

Sally Priesand

First Female Rabbi in the United States, 1946–

On June 3, 1972, a young woman stood on the pulpit at Cincinnati, Ohio's magnificent Plum Street Temple. The president of the Reform seminary blessed Sally and declared her a rabbi. Thirty-five other rabbis were ordained that day, but only Sally made history. In the 2,000 years that rabbis existed, Sally was the first woman known to be ordained.

Sally grew up in a Cleveland household that was more culturally than religiously Jewish. Sally decided at age 16 to become a rabbi. There was one challenge: no seminaries admitted girls into their programs. Luckily, Sally was accepted to Hebrew Union College-Jewish Institute of Religion in 1968—just as the school decided to admit female rabbinic students. "I had no desire to be a pioneer. I just wanted to be a rabbi. And I certainly didn't start out to attract a lot of attention, although that inevitably happened," says Sally.

Some professors and classmates thought her interest was a passing fancy. Others assumed she was there to find a husband. The seminary's dean worried aloud about Sally balancing the rabbinate with motherhood. Finding a congregation willing to consider hiring a woman was challenging. She was the last one in her class to find a position. Sally spent seven years as an assistant and then associate rabbi at Stephen S. Wise Free Synagogue, a large congregation in New York City. But when the senior rabbi retired, the congregation was not ready to hire a woman to take his place.

Finding a new pulpit was very difficult. She took a part-time position and even considered leaving the rabbinate. Finally, Sally found a position at a midsize congregation, Monmouth Reform Temple in Tinton Falls, New Jersey. Sally thrived as their rabbi for 25 years. "I thought that a bigger congregation was the measure of a rabbi's success, and that as the first woman to be ordained, it was almost my obligation to go that route. But fortunately, my own congregation has taught me otherwise," says Sally.

Finding a congregational home for herself, Sally tried to pave an easier path for others. She advocated for more female professors at her seminary, for more women on Jewish governing boards, and especially for fairer practices in hiring. Fifty years after Sally's ordination, close to 1,500 female rabbis serve congregations worldwide. "I did open doors," Sally admits. "But I also held the doors open for those who came after me."

Everybody thought Sally Priesand was the first female rabbi, until they learned about . . .

Regina Jonas

Trailblazing Rabbi, Hidden & Forgotten, 1902–1944

When the Berlin Wall separating East and West Berlin came down in 1989, a long-lost Jewish archive was discovered in East Germany. The archive contained letters, sermons, photographs, and a certificate of ordination not seen for nearly 50 years. Most people had thought Sally Priesand was the world's first female rabbi. But some of the papers belonged to a woman named Regina Jonas, who was ordained 37 years before Sally.

Regina came from a poor family. Her father died when she was just nine years old. Regina attended a school for Jewish girls. Even as a young girl, Regina told her classmates she wanted to be a rabbi. After getting a teaching degree, she studied at a liberal Jewish seminary in Berlin. All the other female students at the seminary wanted to be teachers; only Regina wanted to be ordained as a rabbi. She wrote her thesis on the question: "May a woman hold rabbinic office?" It began, "I personally love this profession and, if ever possible, I also want to practice it."

Most of Regina's professors were in favor of her ordination. But the head of school was against it. Regina searched for five years for a rabbi willing to ordain her. Finally, Rabbi Dr. Max Dienemann agreed. On December 27, 1935, Regina became the world's first female rabbi. By then, the Nazis had come to power in Germany. Regina began her rabbinic career as a counselor, working with the Jewish community's neediest members. But as the Nazis imprisoned more of her male colleagues, Regina was invited to preach at Berlin's synagogues, including the grand Neue Synagogue. Regina started traveling to communities across Germany to lead services and preach. Even when the Nazis forced her to do factory work, Regina led services and taught in the factories.

In 1942, the Nazis deported Regina to the concentration camp Theresienstadt. For two years, she served as a rabbi there. In the fall of 1944, the Nazis deported Regina and her mother to Auschwitz. Both women were sent to the gas chambers and killed on the day they arrived. Several of Regina's fellow rabbis survived the Holocaust and knew about her ordination and accomplishments. But they never mentioned her ordination and no one knows why. Finally, when her archives were discovered, the world learned about Regina.

The actress who played Regina Jonas in a movie starred in another movie as . . .

Deborah Lipstadt

AMBASSADOR & HOLOCAUST HISTORIAN, 1947–

When Deborah chose to study for a doctorate in Jewish history, her career path seemed clear. She would become a professor, researching the past, publishing articles and teaching at a university. Although a quiet lifestyle, it would be meaningful and gratifying. Indeed, after she got her degree from Brandeis, Deborah taught at several universities before settling in at Emory in Atlanta. Then her career became far more action-packed and controversial than Deborah ever imagined.

It all began when two colleagues came to Deborah and suggested she research "Holocaust revision" or "Holocaust denial"—a movement that claims the Holocaust never occurred or that trivializes its severity. At first, Deborah laughed. She thought Holocaust denial was a fringe theory and not worth the time to investigate. But then she did some research. Deborah was stunned. Holocaust denial was both mainstream and widespread. Holocaust deniers built their fake arguments on age-old antisemitic stereotypes.

Deborah wrote *Denying the Holocaust*, a book about her findings. Meant to be the conclusion of her research, the book was actually just the beginning. In the book, Deborah calls a British revisionist historian named David Irving a Holocaust denier. Unhappy with the characterization, David Irving sued Deborah in the British courts for libel, or publishing false and damaging statements. Deborah hired a team of top lawyers and historians to fight the suit.

The case lasted six years and cost $1.5 million for Deborah's defense, money largely donated by Deborah's supporters. Three thousand pages of testimony were submitted. In the end, the judge agreed with Deborah, saying John Irving "is an active Holocaust denier; that he is antisemitic and racist and that he associates with right wing extremists who promote neo-Nazism."

After the trial, Deborah wrote another book: *History on Trial: My Day in Court with a Holocaust Denier*. The book was made into a movie entitled *Denial* starring actress Rachel Weisz as Deborah. David Irving had tried to silence Deborah with his lawsuit, but instead it amplified Deborah's message.

In 2022, the Senate confirmed Deborah as the Special Envoy to Monitor and Combat Antisemitism. Instead of Professor Lipstadt, she is now Ambassador Lipstadt. In her new role, she travels the world to support U.S. foreign policy to fight antisemitism.

Her quiet, academic life didn't exactly go as planned.

Deborah Lipstadt serves as a United States ambassador. So did . . .

David Saperstein

Rabbi Lobbyist of Capitol Hill, 1947–

The year was 1969. David, a senior at Cornell University, watched his campus unravel into chaos. Someone put a wooden cross on the porch of a dorm for African American women and set it on fire. In protest, Afro-American Society (AAS) members occupied the student union. They threw everyone else out and padlocked the door. In response, members of a white fraternity tried to take the building back by force. A fight broke out and, fearful of reprisals, the AAS armed itself with rifles and shotguns.

That evening, 6,500 students gathered in the school's arena. David, already known as a campus activist against the Vietnam War, was invited to speak to the gathered students. David thought of his father, a rabbi, and civil rights activist, speaking from a synagogue pulpit to inspire others. Offering words of support, promoting activism, and asking for peace, David helped heal his campus. "Suddenly the power of the spoken word as a way of opening people's thinking and shaping their priorities dawned on me," says David.

David went on to rabbinical school, and later to law school. He believed that the law and the rabbinate would best help him make a positive impact on society and people in need. Since then, David has given eloquent, fiery speeches about civil rights, religious freedom, economic justice, gun control, and more, in front of Congress, presidents, rallies, foreign dignitaries, and in synagogues around the world.

David served as director of the Religious Action Center of Reform Judaism (RAC) in Washington, DC, for over 30 years. Under David's leadership, the RAC became one of Washington's most powerful religious advocacy groups. David retired from the RAC only when President Barack Obama appointed him U.S. Ambassador for International Religious Freedom—the first person of a faith group other than Christianity to hold this post. As Ambassador, David traveled to 32 different countries, working with governments and religious leaders to foster religious freedom around the globe.

Intense and quick-thinking, with a legendary amount of energy, David shares a deep optimism that each person can make a difference. "We may indeed face perilous and unprecedented problems, but paradoxically, we may well be the first generation of Jews living in a world capable of creating the kind of just, peaceful, and compassionate society our history and our values charge us to build."

David Saperstein worked with . . .

Lynne Landsberg

Rabbi & Disability Advocate, 1951–2018

Dazzling. Chic. Cool. A wicked sense of humor. Usually, such words aren't used to describe rabbis. But people used them to describe Lynne. While studying at Harvard Divinity School, Lynne decided to become a rabbi. She loved people, Jewish texts, and social justice. It seemed like a perfect match. Plus, Lynne had style. After ordination, she appeared on *The Today Show* and in *Cosmopolitan Magazine*.

In 1987, Rabbi David Saperstein called Lynne and offered her the job of Associate Director of the Religious Action Center (RAC). Lynne jumped at the opportunity. One of Lynne's first priorities was advocating for the Americans with Disabilities Act (ADA), which prohibits discrimination based on disability. Ironically and tragically, 12 years later, Lynne herself became disabled and needed the ADA to guarantee her rights.

On a snowy Sunday morning in 1999, Lynne was driving her son to synagogue. Her Jeep skidded on a patch of black ice and hit a tree. Thankfully, her son escaped uninjured, but Lynne suffered a traumatic brain injury and fell into a deep coma. The doctors warned she might never wake up. Six weeks later, she opened her eyes. Lynne had to relearn everything: how to walk, talk, eat, and even simple things like her favorite colors. But her sense of humor and sense of justice never died; both came right back. "I've been told that in my former life, I was an effortless multi-tasker, a fast-talker and a quick thinker. I had speaking engagements across the country and composed my most powerful speeches in airplanes and taxis. In my former life, I was Rabbi Lynne Landsberg. And although I am still Rabbi Lynne Landsberg, the rest has changed," said Lynne.

Now that she used a wheelchair or cane, Lynne realized she was treated differently. Store clerks ignored her. Waiters talked to her husband or nurse, not her. Lynne often felt invisible and excluded. The ADA only solved part of the problem of discrimination. Lynne says, "I realized that I had a much bigger job to do." Although working at a much slower pace than before, Lynne devoted herself to advocating for disability inclusion. Over the next several years, she cofounded the Jewish Disability Network and Hineinu: Jewish Community for People of All Abilities.

Faced with seemingly insurmountable challenges, Lynne never gave up. Instead, she became an inspiring voice for inclusion. Dazzling. Chic. Disabled.

Lynne Landsberg worked in a building named for . . .

Kivie Kaplan

Civil Rights Activist & NAACP President, 1904–1975

Kivie always smiled. He believed that by smiling, he could get people to talk about difficult things. No matter where he went or who he met, Kivie handed out cards that said, "Keep Smiling."

Kivie and his two brothers worked hard with their parents in the family leather factory. His parents had emigrated from Lithuania to Boston before Kivie was born. When their parents retired, Kivie and his brothers took over the business. Kivie and his brothers shared their profits with the workers, asked them for suggestions, and provided a free lunch every day. Kivie thought he would be satisfied by making nice leather goods and treating his workers with respect. But working in the factory wasn't enough for Kivie. He wanted to help more people and have a bigger impact on the world.

Kivie saw that people weren't always treated equally. He had experienced prejudice himself. When Kivie got married and went to Florida on his honeymoon, a country club wouldn't let him in because he was Jewish. Signs outside said, "No Jews, no dogs." The club also excluded his driver—an African American man. When this happened, Kivie did not smile. Prejudice made him sad and angry.

So Kivie devoted himself to help stop discrimination. He wanted to make sure all people had equal access to good housing, jobs, and the right to vote. Kivie marched in Selma, Alabama, with Rev. Dr. Martin Luther King, Jr., and went to jail with him. Then Kivie went to Mississippi at a time known as Freedom Summer and helped Black people register to vote.

Kivie volunteered to work with the National Association of Colored People (now called the NAACP). He traveled all over the country, especially in the South, to get people to join the NAACP. It was unusual for a white person to lead an organization for Black people. He grew the organization from 221 members to 53,000 and became its president. This made Kivie smile.

Kivie and his brothers' leather business was very successful. Kivie decided to share his wealth with organizations that meant something to him. He helped purchase the building for the Religious Action Center, where both David Saperstein and Lynne Landsberg worked.

As NAACP president, Kivie met with lots of interesting people, including President John F. Kennedy. Kivie gave the president a card that said, "Keep Smiling." That made President Kennedy laugh. And it made Kivie happy.

Kivie Kaplan attended the 1963 March on Washington. So did . . .

Bob Dylan

Legendary Folk-Rock Songwriter & Singer, 1941–

Guitar slung across his back, 16-year-old Bobby Zimmerman climbed onto the roof of his cabin at Camp Herzl in Wisconsin. There, Bobby belted out songs by his favorite rock musicians. Nobody told him to get down, not even the camp rabbis. They were enjoying his music too much. That summer, Bobby told his bunkmates that he would grow up to be a rock star. They quietly laughed at him.

Bobby started at the University of Minnesota but spent more time performing at coffeehouses than attending class. Coffeehouse audiences wanted folk music, not rock. They thought folk music had more political and spiritual depth. Bobby lasted only a year in college, just long enough for his music to evolve from rock to folk and for him to change his name. The name "Bobby Zimmerman" didn't have star quality. "Bob Dylan" was born. Then he hitched a ride to New York City's Greenwich Village.

In New York, success came quickly. He signed with Columbia Records. His songs like "Blowin' in the Wind" and "The Times They Are A-Changin'" soon became civil rights anthems. Although he found fame with folk music, rock and roll's strong beat, catchy melodies, and electric sound still spoke to him. He wondered: Did music need to be folk or rock? Couldn't it be a blend of each?

The 1965 Newport Music Festival was a turning point. Fans came to the festival expecting him to play acoustic guitar, the main instrument of folk musicians. But Bob had never cared much for other people's expectations. Bob and his band came onstage with electric instruments, like rock stars. Half the crowd cheered wildly. The other half booed. Bob realized many fans didn't understand him. He was an artist on a creative journey. He wanted to try different musical styles and merge them to create something meaningful.

In the 60 years since the Newport Music Festival, Bob has performed over 4,000 concerts, written more than 500 songs, and experimented with musical styles from folk to rock to gospel. "This is the flat-out truth: I find the religiosity and philosophy in the music. I don't find it anywhere else," says Bob.

Now in his 80s, Bob still writes music and performs. In 2016, he received the Nobel Prize for Literature for his innovations in songwriting—the only musician ever honored with the prize. Bob didn't attend the awards ceremony. He was on tour, performing.

Bob Dylan got his musical start at a Jewish summer camp.
So did . . .

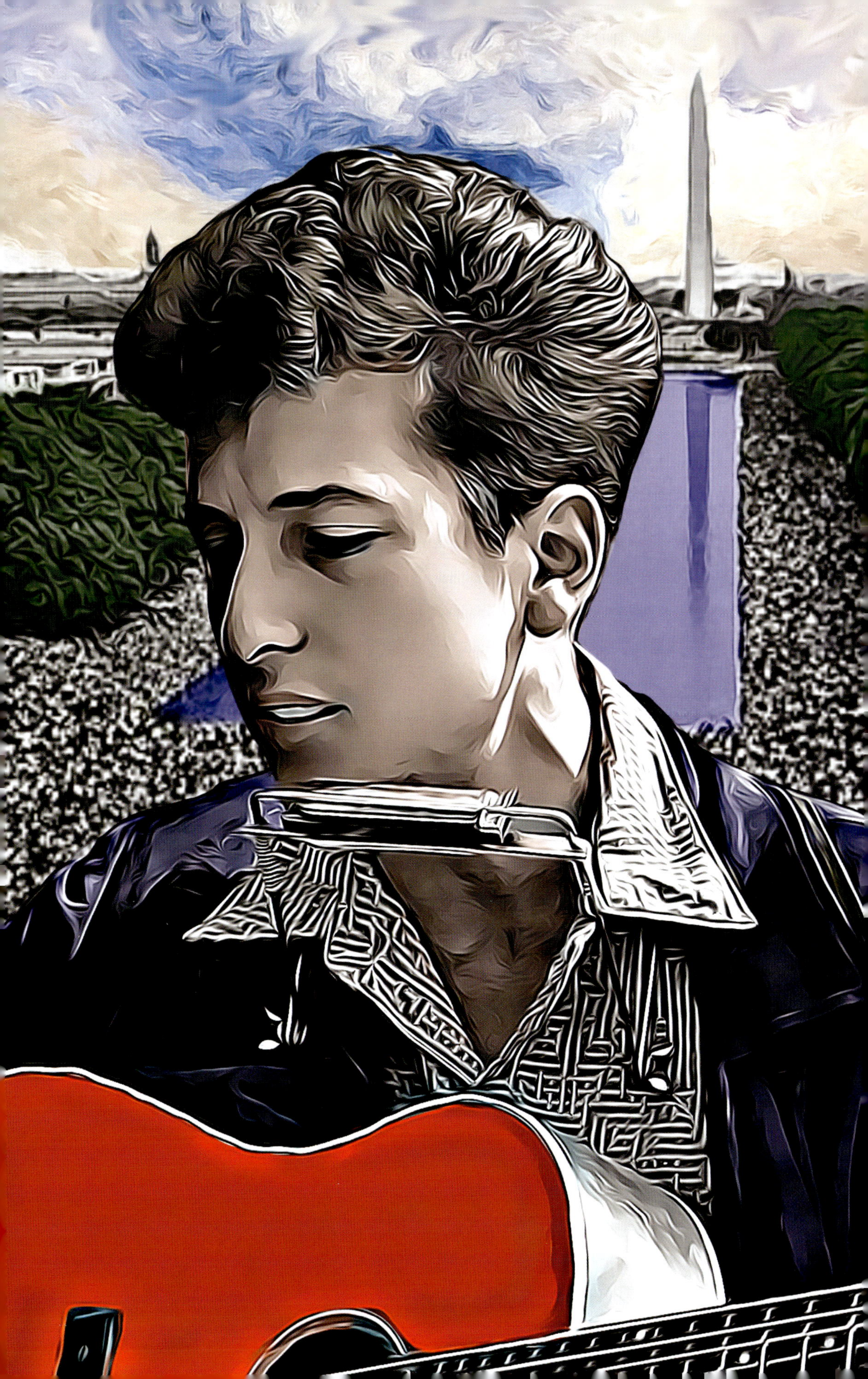

Debbie Friedman

Revolutionary Writer of Jewish Music, 1951–2011

As a teenager, Debbie was often bored at synagogue. The style of prayer was very different from the folk music that she and her friends listened to. Growing up in St. Paul, Minnesota, in the 1950s and 1960s, she loved how folk music brought people together, making them want to sing. Debbie taught herself to play guitar by listening to her favorite folk musicians.

One Shabbat, Debbie had a revelation: "The rabbi was talking, the choir was singing, and nobody was doing anything. There was no participation."

Not long afterward, a new, unique melody came to her. The melody was catchy, spiritual, and easy to sing. Experimenting, she put verses from the prayer book to the melody and played it for a group of other teenagers. "All of a sudden they stood up, grabbed each other's arms and joined in this prayer," she said. "I realized something powerful was happening."

Debbie Friedman had found her calling.

Soon she began writing music for Jewish summer camps. Campers brought Debbie's melodies back to their synagogues. They demanded that their synagogues have more music like Debbie's songs, so people could sing along. Change can be hard. Not everybody liked Debbie's music. Some saw it as a threat to established cantorial tradition.

Slowly, Debbie's influence revolutionized synagogue music. Her songs became common at Reform, Conservative, and even some Orthodox synagogues, as well as Christian churches. Today, many people who sing her music—songs like "Not by Might" and "Miriam's Song"—don't realize she wrote them.

Debbie published more than 20 albums of Jewish music. Her lyrics are included in a line of Hallmark greeting cards. In 1996, she sang at Carnegie Hall. But rather than performing, she encouraged her audience to sing, giving voice to all who sang with her. She especially incorporated the stories of Jewish women into her songs. Debbie said, "We have to reframe things so that women's voices are heard."

Some of Debbie's most deeply expressed and spiritual music emerged from her own struggle with an illness that afflicted her during the last 20 years of her life. Tragically, Debbie died at age 59. But her music lives on.

Today, synagogue services are far more participatory. And it all began with a girl named Debbie who wanted to sing—and help others sing, too—because she felt alone in prayer in the synagogue.

Debbie Friedman was influenced by . . .

Leonard Cohen

Poetic Songwriter, Soulful Singer, 1934–2016

Leonard owned dozens of notebooks—leather-covered journals, reporters' pads, diaries. He filled each one with draft lyrics for his music, especially for one song, "Hallelujah." In "Hallelujah," Leonard tells stories of love and passion, including the biblical tale of King David and Bathsheba. Over 10 years, Leonard wrote 80 draft verses for "Hallelujah." Taking his time to write didn't bother him. He saw songwriting as a spiritual experience. "If I knew where these songs come from, I'd go there more often," said Leonard.

When Leonard finally finished "Hallelujah," he eagerly shared it with Columbia Records, his record label. But Columbia rejected it. Devastated, Leonard signed with a small record label to record his song. Slowly, other artists, including Bob Dylan, began singing "Hallelujah." Leonard saw the song as his spiritual gift to others. In 2001, the directors of the movie *Shrek* used "Hallelujah" in a key scene. Nearly overnight, "Hallelujah" became a classic. Since then, over 300 different artists have released their own versions of "Hallelujah," in languages ranging from Hebrew to Filipino to German.

Leonard's love of music and poetry began by listening to his mother sing in their Montreal home. As a college student, Leonard published his first poems. After college, Leonard lived in Toronto, New York, and London. He studied law, then literature, but kept returning to poetry. He moved to the Greek island of Hydras. There, he rented a place for $14 a month, wrote his first novels, and turned his attention to songwriting. When he felt ready, he moved back to New York.

For nearly 50 years, Leonard wrote soulful, realistic songs about life: love and hate, war and peace, ecstasy and depression. Leonard toured the world with his music, including several visits to Israel. Leonard incorporated Judaism and many other spiritual traditions into his music. Exploring other religions "enriched my understanding of my own tradition," said Leonard.

Leonard gave his notebooks to the University of Toronto, a natural choice for a proud Canadian. "I have a deep tribal sense," he said. "I grew up in a synagogue that my ancestors built."

The month before his death, Leonard released his final album. On the title track, he asked the cantor from his childhood synagogue to chant the biblical word *Hineni*—"Here I am."

Leonard Cohen, the bohemian songwriter, had come home.

Leonard Cohen lived in Greece. So did . . .

Albert Bourla

Pfizer CEO During the Covid Epidemic, 1961–

As a boy, Albert tried to imagine his hometown of Salonica, Greece, before World War II. He pictured the port city with synagogues full of people, crowded Jewish bakeries, and busy kosher butcher shops. But Albert had to push his imagination hard to picture 50,000 Jews living in Salonica. He never would meet most of them. During World War II, the Nazis deported most Jews in Salonica to concentration camps. Only 2,000 survived. Albert's parents were among the lucky ones.

Many Holocaust survivors chose not to tell their children about their experiences. It was just too painful. But Albert's parents wanted him and his sister to know what happened. Albert says, "They wanted us to remember. To remember all the lives that were lost. To remember what can happen when the virus of evil is allowed to spread unchecked. But, most important, to remember the value of a human life."

Even though Albert's parents had suffered during the war, they taught him to approach life with a positive attitude. "The way that their stories were always ending was a celebration of life: 'Look at us, we're alive. We were almost dead and we're alive. Life is wonderful.'"

Protecting human life became Albert's mission. Albert has a scientist's mind. At university, he studied biotechnology. Then he went to work at Pfizer, an international company that creates new vaccines and medicines. Albert worked very hard for Pfizer and, over the years, took on more and more important roles. In 2019, just as the Covid-19 pandemic began, Albert was promoted to lead the whole company. Albert pushed the other scientists at Pfizer to work hard and quickly to develop a vaccine. Albert emphasized teamwork to his researchers. They collaborated with Israeli researchers and others around the world on the vaccine. Vaccines often take years to develop, but Pfizer developed a Covid-19 vaccine in under a year.

In 2022, Albert received the Genesis Prize, sometimes called the Jewish Nobel Prize, given to a Jewish person who has made a unique contribution to the world. At the award ceremony, Albert offered this piece of advice: "Try to stay as united as you can, and don't let small things divide you."

What will Albert do with the million dollars in prize money? He plans to fund a Holocaust Museum Memorial in Salonica.

Albert Bourla took a lead in developing an important vaccine. So did . . .

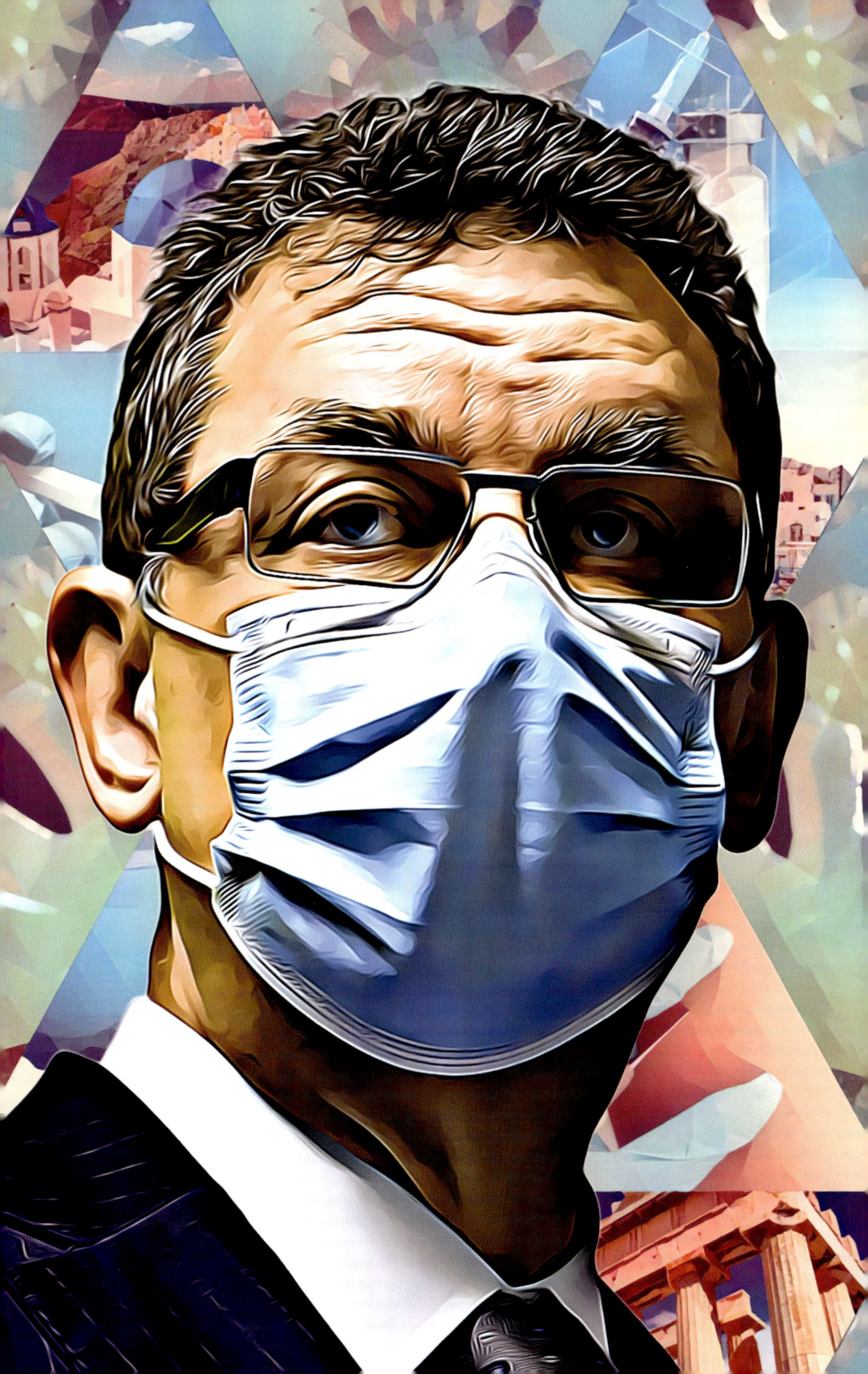

Jonas Salk

Scientist who Developed the Polio Vaccine, 1914–1995

Jonas arranged the supplies on the countertop in his family's kitchen: syringes, needles, and precious vials of vaccine. He boiled water and sterilized the needles. Gently, Jonas injected each child and his wife in their arms. His eldest son Peter said it barely hurt at all. Good. But Jonas would not sleep well for the next three weeks, until he was certain that the vaccine hadn't given polio to his family.

Growing up in New York City, the son of Russian Jewish immigrants, Jonas lived through polio epidemics. During the early 20th century, the virus struck in the summer, infecting as many as a half million people each year, causing muscle weakening, and sometimes paralysis and even death. Most polio victims were infants and young children. Parents and children lived in fear of the next epidemic.

As a medical researcher, Jonas had devoted many years to fighting polio. It had not always been easy. Although a brilliant student, Jonas struggled to find a research position because he was Jewish. Jonas' mentor in medical school had to vouch for him, writing a recommendation that ended: "Dr. Salk is a member of the Jewish race but has, I believe, a very great capacity to get on with people."

Now, finally, after many false starts, Jonas had developed a vaccine with extraordinary promise. He had tested his vaccine on lab animals and on patients who already had polio. None contracted the disease, and all showed increased immunity. Before sharing the vaccine with the world, he had wanted to test the vaccine's safety one more time. His family and a few lab workers bravely volunteered.

The weeks after injecting his family passed slowly. Jonas watched for symptoms of disease. None came. But had the vaccine worked? When Jonas tested their blood, the news was good—wonderful, in fact. His sons, his wife, and the lab workers all had immunity without contracting the disease. Jonas had found a way to prevent polio.

Soon after, one million healthy children received the polio vaccine in an enormous drug trial. They were called "Polio Pioneers." By 1959, the polio vaccine was available in 90 countries and within 25 years, polio no longer existed in most of the world. Jonas chose not to submit a patent application for the vaccine. The vaccine became his gift to the world.

Jonas Salk created a vaccine for polio,
a disease that impaired . . .

VACCINE WORKS!
SALK POLIO
VACCINE
EFFECT
OLIO VACCINE
TRAI SALK SUCCESS

Frida Kahlo

Mexican Artist & Political Radical, 1907–1954

Many months had passed since the bus accident, but Frida still was in a full body cast. She lay in bed, an artist's canvas resting on her stomach. Before the accident, the 17-year-old's life revolved around school, friends, and political activism. Now this had become Frida's world: a four-poster bed, a bowl of paintbrushes, and a mirror hanging on the canopy above, reflecting back her own image. Frida refused to let the pain debilitate her. She had already overcome polio as a young child. Her body might be injured, but her creative spirit certainly was not.

Frida dipped a brush into paint. She peered into the mirror above her and imagined herself surrounded by lush tropical trees. Then she began to paint her own image. From bed, she flourished as an artist, honing the skills that eventually made her one of Mexico's most celebrated painters. Her painting explored what it meant to be a woman, a Mexican, a political liberal, a person in pain, and a person passionately in love. As time went on, Frida began to recognize another identity within herself—a Jewish one. Frida's mother had Spanish and indigenous Mexican ancestry. Her father came from Europe. Frida said he was a Hungarian Jew.

Some contemporary scholars question her Jewish lineage. They say Frida's father wasn't Jewish. So why, then, would Frida claim to be a Jew? That's something of a mystery. One thing is certain: Frida felt a kinship with the Jewish people and had many close Jewish friends.

Although the Nazis posed no direct threat to Frida in Mexico, Frida watched with disgust as they came to power. As the Nazis tightened their grip on Europe, Frida had a choice: she could ignore Nazi injustice halfway around the world or she could speak out, starting with declaring her Jewish identity. Frida embraced Judaism.

Frida incorporated Jewish symbols and themes into her art as a form of protest. In one painting, Frida shows her Jewish and non-Jewish ancestors organized as a family tree. The Nazis used similar charts to identify and persecute Jews. In another painting, Frida shows scenes from the biblical story of Moses with a portrait of Hitler alongside Pharoah.

Certainly, Frida didn't stop the Nazis by identifying as Jewish. But with her boundless creativity and passion, Frida took one small step against hate. And small steps make a difference.

Frida Kahlo learned to draw while recovering in bed.
So did . . .

Maurice Sendak

Children's Illustrator & Author, 1928–2012

"And Max, the king of all wild things, was lonely and wanted to be where someone loved him best of all." —*Where the Wild Things Are*

Maurice didn't have an easy childhood. Sadness often filled his family's Brooklyn, New York, apartment. Maurice's parents had emigrated from Poland, leaving many relatives behind. Most were killed during the Holocaust. This horror left a deep shadow on Maurice.

A sickly child, Maurice spent long hours in bed. He entertained himself by reading, drawing, and looking out the window. Comic books and novels like *Huckleberry Finn* and *Tom Sawyer* were his companions. At age 12, Maurice went with his family to see *Fantasia*, Disney's classic animated film. He was mesmerized. By the end of the movie, he knew he wanted to be an illustrator.

Maurice got his start as a freelance artist, illustrating other authors' books. Then he began writing and illustrating his own stories. Over his 60-year career, Maurice illustrated over 150 children's books, including the beloved classic *Where the Wild Things Are*. At that time, most children's books were simplistic, with well-behaved children and almost no conflict. Maurice took a revolutionary approach when writing his own books. "Children who fight back, children who are full of excitement are the kind of children I like," said Maurice.

Thinking back to his own childhood, he wrote stories about resilience and facing fears. His stories had emotional honesty, passion, and humor, and his artwork was fanciful and sometimes dark. "Children are tough, though we tend to think of them as fragile. They have to be tough. Childhood is not easy," said Maurice. "We sentimentalize children, but they know what's real and what's not."

His approach to storytelling influenced the future of children's literature. He's been called the most important children's author of the 20th century. But Maurice was forever modest. He said, "My work is not great, but it's respectable. I have no false illusions."

Maurice didn't avoid tough topics in his writing, but he had one rule: his stories had to end safely, with his characters finding security, love, and acceptance.

"The wild things roared their terrible roars and gnashed their terrible teeth and rolled their terrible eyes and showed their terrible claws but Max stepped into his private boat and waved good-bye." —*Where the Wild Things Are*

Maurice Sendak worked on Sesame Street's early development. Who appeared with the Muppets?

Stan Lee

Writer, Editor & Publisher at Marvel Comics, 1922–2018

As a boy growing up in New York City, Stan read constantly—*The Hardy Boys*, Charles Dickens, Mark Twain, Sherlock Holmes, and more. Whenever he got 50 cents, he would buy a book. He read so much that his mother gave him a book stand to use while he ate dinner. Stan's parents, immigrants from Romania, struggled during the Great Depression. Stan used reading to escape the stress at home.

As he grew up, Stan started envisioning himself as a writer. He hoped that, someday, he might write the great American novel. The *New York Herald Tribune* sponsored a weekly writing contest for teenagers. Stan won so many times that the newspaper suggested he become a professional writer. That validation changed his life. When it came time to get a job, Stan knew traditional book publishing was often closed to Jews. So, Stan used comics as his superpower.

At age 17, with his uncle's help, Stan got a job filling inkwells and fetching coffee at Timely Comics, which later became Marvel. Knowing that great writers often had pen names, Stan divided his first name into two—"Stanley" became "Stan Lee." His first writing assignment was *Captain America*. The editor liked Stan's work and gave him more stories to write. Even while serving in the Army during World War II, Stan submitted comic texts weekly to Marvel. Stan rose quickly through the ranks at Marvel, eventually becoming editor-in-chief. He brought to life comic book heroes like Spiderman, Black Widow, Hulk, and Black Panther. His contributions transformed Marvel into a major cultural force.

When Stan started in comics, superheroes were nearly perfect humans. Stan changed that. He gave them quirks and imperfections. He thought that vulnerabilities made the characters more interesting to readers. He also worked to have diverse characters: "We live in a diverse society—in fact, a diverse world—and we must learn to live in peace and with respect for each other."

Although not religious, Stan's Jewish values molded his characters. "You can wrap all of Judaism up in one sentence, and that is, 'Do not do unto others. . . ,'" said Stan. "All I tried to do in my stories was show that there's some innate goodness in the human condition. And there's going to be evil; we should always be fighting evil."

As a child, Stan dreamed of writing the great American novel. Through comics, he did.

Stan Lee's Captain America memorialized . . .

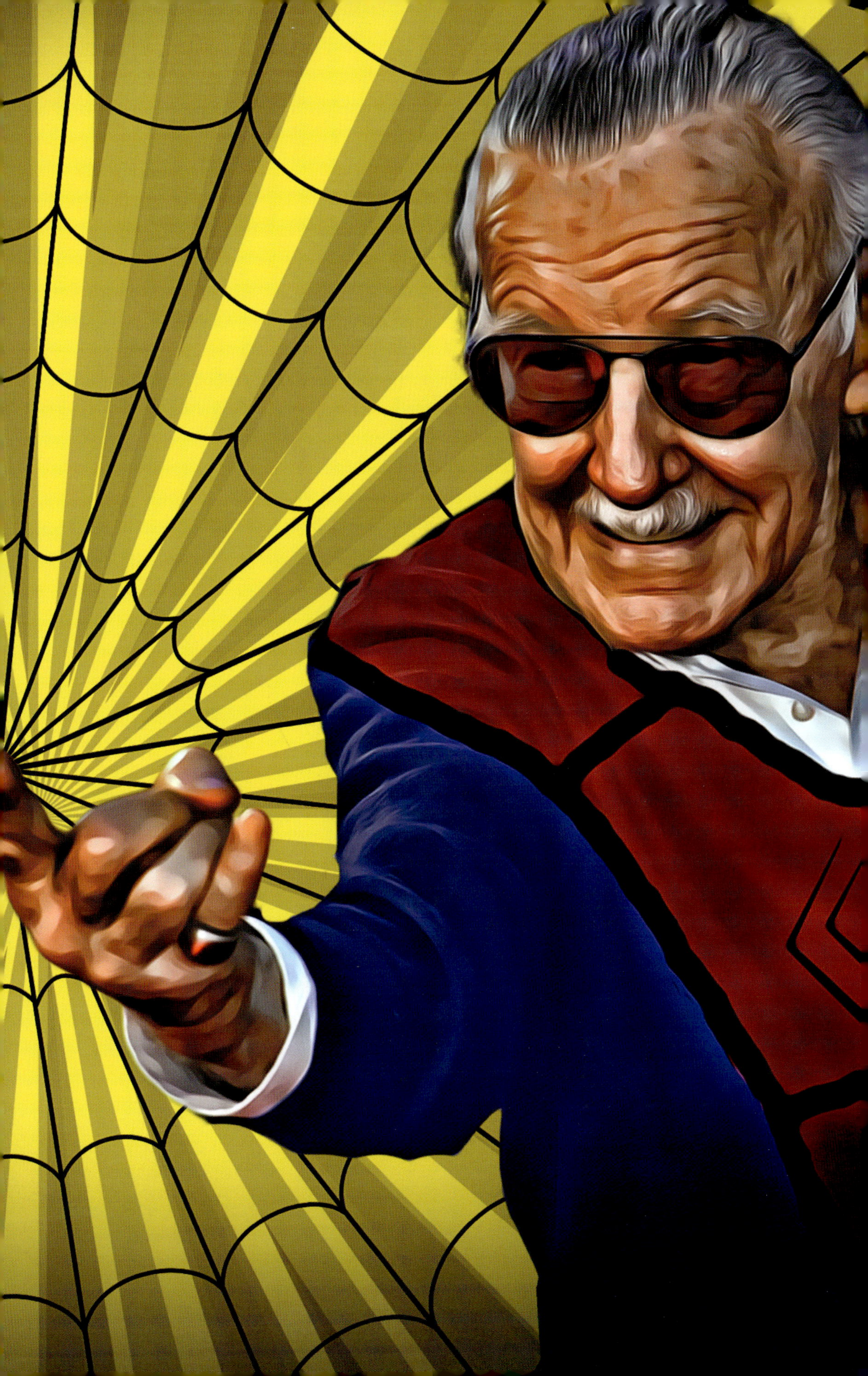

Judith Resnik

NASA Astronaut, 1949–1986

On the far side of the moon, there is a small crate. The crater has a name: Resnik. And it has a story. Judith Resnik grew up in Akron, Ohio, but was destined for places much farther away. She graduated first in her high school class. She earned a perfect score on her college entrance exams. Her high school classmates voted her runner-up for Homecoming Queen. Friends described her as driven, funny, and inquisitive. She played piano so well that Juilliard, the most prestigious music school in the country, accepted her. When asked about her intensity playing the piano, Judith said, "I never play anything softly."

Judith turned down Juilliard and decided to study electrical engineering instead. After college, Judith continued her studies and earned a PhD. In 1978, NASA started recruiting women for their Astronaut Corps. Although Judith had never been particularly interested in the space program, she saw it as the ultimate challenge. "She was looking for a purpose in life," says her father. Eight thousand women applied for the program. Only six women were chosen. Judith was one of them.

In September 1984, Judith became the second woman and the first American Jew to go into space. Judith didn't like such designations. She told her father, "Dad, I don't want to be a Jewish astronaut, I don't want to be a Jewish woman astronaut, I just want to be an astronaut, period. I just want to go out in space and do my job."

Her job was operating the space shuttle's robotic arm. From space, Judith held a sign that read "Hi Dad" and told President Ronald Reagan, "The Earth looks great." When asked about the dangers of space travel, Judith said, "it does not enter any of our minds that we're doing something dangerous."

On January 28, 1986, Judith went into space for a second time. She and six other crew members blasted off from Cape Canaveral in the Space Shuttle Challenger. Seventy-three seconds into the flight, Challenger exploded and broke apart, killing everybody aboard.

One thousand people attended Judith's funeral at her childhood synagogue. The International Astronomical Union named the impact crater on the moon in her memory. Judith's life was tragically short, but her impact was intense on earth and beyond.

Instead of engineering school, Judith Resnik considered studying piano at Juilliard. Who taught at Juilliard?

NASA
JUDY RESNIK
JSC HOUSTON

Anna Sokolow

Dancer, Choreographer & Activist, 1910-2000

On the Lower East Side of New York, Anna sat in class, daydreaming about dancing. She didn't like to sit still at a desk. She didn't like to focus on her teacher's endless lessons. She wanted to take a dance lesson at the Henry Street Settlement House or rehearse at the Neighborhood Playhouse. Her parents, though, had different plans for her. A new immigrant from Russia, her mother toiled in the Lower East Side's sweatshops while caring for Anna's ailing father at home and organizing a labor union for garment workers. Her parents impressed on Anna: Study hard in school and make a better life for yourself. But Anna just wanted to dance. She had fallen "madly in love with dancing" at age 10 and wanted to do nothing else.

By age 15, Anna had had enough with school. She wanted to learn, just not in a classroom. Clashing with her parents, she dropped out and left home to be a dancer. She danced as much as she could and supported herself by working in a factory, tying tea bags. By 1930, Anna was dancing as a soloist with the prestigious Martha Graham dance company. Martha Graham herself became Anna's mentor.

But after eight years, Anna and Martha clashed on what dance meant and Anna left to start her own company. Anna believed dance was not just entertainment; it could also explore pressing contemporary issues—from the Depression to the Holocaust to workers' rights. She remembered her mother working long hours in a garment factory. She wanted to use dance to share this experience with the world. Anna belonged to the Radical Dance Movement. Its motto: "Dance is a weapon in the class struggle."

Anna traveled frequently to Mexico and Israel to bring modern dance to those countries. Anna incorporated Jewish stories and rituals, like the wedding ceremony, into her choreography.

The girl who never liked school became a teacher. For 25 years, she taught at Juilliard, the premier performing arts school in the United States. Anna was known as a strict teacher with high standards. She encouraged her students to display deeper emotion through dance. She'd often clap her hands and yell, "No, I don't believe it!" at her students to inspire them to work harder. She told her students: "I don't dislike you; that's not why I'm hard on you. But I love dance more than I love you."

Anna Sokolow protested the Vietnam War. So did . . .

Bella Abzug

Congresswoman & Ardent Feminist, 1920–1998

In 1950, Bella, a young New York attorney, traveled to Mississippi to defend a Black man—a dangerous business in that era. Local editorial writers threatened her defendant with lynching. The police followed Bella, and not to protect her. She refused to be scared off. For her safety, Bella spent the night sleeping upright in a brightly lit bus station. "That woman has more guts than the whole Army," said her husband, Martin. Bella was eight months pregnant at the time.

Some say that Bella was "born yelling." Growing up on the streets of the Bronx in New York, she was a champion marbles player, graffiti artist, musician, and, also, a proud Zionist. By age 11, she and her friends were giving speeches at subway stations to raise money for Israel. Bella soon earned the nickname "Battling Bella."

Bella adored her father, an outspoken Russian immigrant who encouraged her activism. He owned a butcher shop named the Live and Let Live Meat Market. When Bella was 13, her father died. Bella pledged to honor him by saying kaddish at their Orthodox synagogue. But the synagogue leaders said only sons could recite kaddish. Bella defied those leaders and, for a year, attended synagogue each morning before school to recite kaddish. Later in life, she advised others to be bold: "People may not like it, but no one will stop you."

Bella attended law school at a time when few women became lawyers. Her reputation for being tough, combative, and industrious grew there. She used the law to advocate for civil rights, workers, the disenfranchised, women, the LGBTQ community, and the environment. And she spoke out forcefully against nuclear weapons and the war in Vietnam.

In 1970, Bella ran for Congress. Her slogan: "This woman's place is in the house—The House of Representatives." Bella won. In Congress, she dismissed so-called "rules" about seniority and the like. On her first day in office, she introduced legislation to withdraw American troops from Vietnam. She fiercely advocated for the Equal Rights Amendment.

Early on, Bella understood that she needed to be noticed in order to make a difference. She began wearing large, stylish hats. Her hats became her trademark. When elected to Congress, the leadership said hats weren't allowed in the House Chamber. Of course, Bella didn't listen. She simply responded, "It's what's under the hat that counts!"

Bella Abzug served in Congress. So does . . .

ABZUG-
lutely
LIFE
WOMEN IN
POLITICS
How are they doing?
Where are they going?
Bella
Bella for senate

Jamie Raskin

Congressman & Constitutional Attorney, 1962–

Jamie's first real memory takes place in a courtroom. When Jamie was six years old, his father stood trial for criminal conspiracy. His father wasn't a hardened criminal, but a protestor against the Vietnam War. He and four other men were accused of encouraging young people to avoid the military draft and burn their draft cards. As Jamie sat in court and watched his father's trial, he worried that his father might go to jail. Even after his father was acquitted, the trial confused and intrigued Jamie. He says, "It launched my lifelong fascination with the law and showed me how law can be an instrument to hurt people and injure people but also an instrument to help and free them."

Growing up outside Washington, DC, Jamie's interest in the law, history, and politics only grew. He was so fascinated by constitutional law that he composed a constitution for his high school's student body. After high school, Jamie went to Harvard University and then Harvard Law School. For more than 25 years, Jamie taught constitutional law, then decided to run for office. After serving as a Maryland state senator for three terms, Jamie was elected to Congress. Jamie tirelessly advocates for a host of issues including civil rights, free speech, LGBTQ rights, and gun control.

A personal tragedy followed by a national crisis thrust Jamie into the limelight. On New Year's Eve 2020, Jamie's son Tommy died by suicide after a long struggle with depression. The day after Tommy's funeral, Jamie pushed himself to go to Capitol Hill to verify Joe Biden's presidential victory. That afternoon, an angry, violent mob stormed the Capitol. They believed the election had been stolen from Donald Trump. As the mob attacked police officers and ransacked the building, Jamie and the rest of Congress went into hiding.

Afterward Jamie said, "I am not going to lose my son in 2020 and country in 2021." Jamie became the most vocal and visible Congress member to investigate the January 6 attack. He took a leading role in the second impeachment trial of Donald Trump and the congressional inquiry into the insurrection. His impassioned speeches captured the attention of the entire country; his ability to find strength in Tommy's memory became an inspiration. As he says, "If a person can grow through unthinkable trauma and loss, perhaps a nation may, too."

Jamie Raskin was an editor of the Harvard Law Review.
So was . . .

Elena Kagan

Supreme Court Justice, 1960–

Imagine a Saturday night in Manhattan. High school students have gathered for house parties or gone dancing at clubs. Elena, however, sits on the steps of the Metropolitan Museum of Art, talking with friends about student government. If you ask her, she'll say she wants to be a Supreme Court Justice someday. Classmates believe she just might reach that goal. As though to prove the point, in a high school yearbook picture, she wears a judge's robe and holds a gavel. Next to the picture is a quote from Justice Felix Frankfurter, a Jewish member of the Supreme Court.

Like her role model Justice Frankfurter, Elena has never been afraid to share her opinion, advocate for her beliefs, or reach a creative compromise. As a young teen, Elena attended Lincoln Square Synagogue, an Orthodox congregation. Her family wasn't Orthodox, but her mother liked the rabbi there. Yet Elena clashed with him. She wanted to become bat mitzvah. But the congregation only allowed bar mitzvah for boys, not bat mitzvah for girls. Elena negotiated a compromise with the rabbi. The synagogue would celebrate its first "bat Torah." Elena didn't read Torah but read the book of Ruth on a Friday night. "It was sort of a disappointment, because I didn't get to do all the stuff my brother had done," she says. "But I have to say that they came a super long way even to do that."

After her bat Torah celebration, she shared a Shabbat dinner at the congregation with the boy becoming bar mitzvah the next day. The boy's parents were divorced. His grandmothers each insisted he sit at her table at dinner. The boy broke down in tears. Compassionately, Elena consoled him, then came up with a solution. He sat at Elena's table.

Elena attended Princeton, Oxford, and Harvard Law School. She clerked with Justice Thurgood Marshall on the Supreme Court. She served as dean at Harvard Law School and held several high-level positions in President Bill Clinton's administration before being nominated by President Barack Obama to the US Supreme Court. Even with all those accomplishments, she became the youngest justice on the Court when she was confirmed at age 50.

During her confirmation, a conservative senator asked Elena how she spent Christmas. Elena answered, "Like all Jews, I was probably at a Chinese restaurant."

Even as a Supreme Court nominee, Elena was her genuine self—sharp, direct, and proudly Jewish.

Elena Kagan fought for women's rights in Orthodox Judaism. So does . . .

Sara Hurwitz

Groundbreaking Orthodox Rabbinic Leader, 1977–

Like most South Africans before the 1990s, Sara grew up in a segregated world. She only knew one Black person: her family's maid. One morning, her family got lost on the way to a bat mitzvah reception and mistakenly drove into a Black township. Sara saw the poverty and slums around her. Asking her parents about the upsetting experience, she learned they opposed apartheid, the system of laws oppressing Blacks in South Africa. When Sara was 12, her family moved to Florida because they no longer felt they could live in an apartheid state. The apartheid system in South Africa ended three months later.

Sara's family was proudly Jewish but not observant. As she journeyed through public high school and then Barnard College, she immersed herself more in the Orthodox community. Following graduation, she studied at the Drisha Institute in a Talmud and Jewish law program for women. She learned all the same things Orthodox men learn to become rabbis. Sara decided she wanted to fulfill a rabbi's role, even if only men had ever served as Orthodox rabbis. She says a "passion for teaching Torah and serving the Jewish community" inspired her.

Yet her South African upbringing also contributed. Her parents had instilled within her a sense of fairness and equality. "By taking us out of a country that didn't allow people to participate equally in society, that sent a strong message that all people should be able to do what they want, and everybody is created equal," says Sara.

Sara committed herself to finding a way within Orthodox Jewish law for women to fulfill rabbinic roles. In 2009, Sara was ordained by Rabbis Avi Weiss and Daniel Sperber. A few months fter her ordination, Rabbi Weiss gave her the title *rabba*—the feminine equivalent to rabbi. Some people protested vehemently against Sara's ordination. "It was definitely a challenging time in my life," Sara says. "I had a tremendous support system in my family as well in my community."

These days, Sara serves as president of Yeshivat Maharat, a rabbinical school for Orthodox women she helped start. She is frequently listed among the most influential rabbis in the United States.

Although Jewish texts guide her life, Sara also considers Nelson Mandela, the first Black president of South Africa, to be her role model. For inspiration, she thinks of Mandela "marching toward equality and justice and integrity."

Sara Hurwitz grew up in South Africa. So did . . .

Helen Suzman

Legislator who Fought Apartheid, 1917-2009

The police dog snarled at the protestors and pulled on its leash. But Helen would have none of it: not snarling German Shepherds and certainly not apartheid, the laws segregating Black and white people in South Africa. Teeth bared, the dog lunged toward her. Helen, however, would take down the dog and apartheid with one weapon: her voice. Helen commanded: "Sit." With a whimper, the dog sat, disarmed.

As a child, Helen never imagined herself staring down police dogs or protesting in the streets. She grew up privileged, unaware of the poverty plaguing South Africa's Black communities. In college, Helen studied economics and how apartheid functioned. The reality sickened her. Determined not to live in a country with unjust laws, Helen had two options: leave South Africa or advocate for change. South Africa was her home. She ran for public office and won, becoming the only Jewish woman in South Africa's parliament.

In parliament, Helen gave speech after speech against apartheid. The other parliament members interrupted her. They yelled antisemitic rants. They booed. But Helen kept speaking. She spoke at rallies. She spoke on TV. Even after she received threatening phone calls and her tires were slashed, Helen refused to be silent. Even the prime minister tried to scare Helen. She told him, "I am not frightened of you—I never have been, and I never will be."

Helen decided to visit the notorious prison on Robben Island and its most famous prisoner, Nelson Mandela, a Black man imprisoned for speaking against apartheid. Helen took a dismal ferry ride to the island. She walked down the long corridor of prison cells to the last one—Nelson's cell. Putting his hand through the bars, Nelson shook Helen's hand. He said, "How do you do, Mrs. Suzman. I'm very pleased to meet you."

Helen visited Nelson many times and worked hard to get him released. No other parliament member visited Nelson during his 30 years in prison. Finally, apartheid ended. Nelson was elected as South Africa's first Black president. When Nelson signed the new South African constitution, Helen stood by his side. Helen fought hard for equal rights, but she did not take credit for it. Helen, who always spoke up, was quietly satisfied.

Helen Suzman served in a parliament in Africa.
So does . . .

FREE
SOUTH
AFRICA
NOW!

Gershom Sizomu

Ugandan Rabbi & Statesman, 1972–

Born near the city of Mbale in Uganda, Gershom grew up during a terrible time in the country. Idi Amin, a ruthless military dictator, ruled the country. Among his cruel edicts, Idi Amin outlawed Judaism. Idi Amin's henchmen even arrested Gershom's father for building a sukkah. The family paid five goats to have him released. "We went underground," says Gershom. "I learned it is dangerous to be a minority and have no political power. We were not allowed to express our Judaism. Our synagogues were destroyed. No singing Jewish songs, no Sabbath."

On the first night of Passover, 1979, Idi Amin's government was overthrown and freedom of religion was restored. Gershom's family held a Seder for 200 people to celebrate. They had been leaders among the Abayudaya or "children of Judah" since his great-grandfather had founded the community in 1919. At Gershom's bar mitzvah in 1983, his father and grandfather proclaimed him the rabbi of their village in Uganda. As he got older, Gershom decided to truly lead his community; but first, he needed to study. In 2003, Gershom, his wife, and two small children left Uganda for Los Angeles so he could attend rabbinical school. Five years later, he was ordained as a Conservative rabbi, the first native-born Black rabbi in sub-Saharan Africa. He returned to Uganda to lead the Abayudaya.

Along with being a spiritual leader, Gershom focuses on building the community. He opened a yeshiva to train African teachers and rabbis. He also works with many people converting to Judaism, some from other countries like Kenya, Nigeria, and South Africa. The Abayudaya community is now 2,000-3,000 people strong. Gershom says, "The relationship between God and the Jews in the Torah resonates for many spiritual seekers. It is important that Africans and others know that they can choose Judaism as a spiritual path and that we are open to them."

In 2016, following a hotly contested race, Gershom won a seat in Uganda's parliament. Gershom said this will "be the first time our community of Ugandan Jews will be represented. Now they will see that we exist, that we are participating in our country's development and growth." When he was elected, he was given an allowance to purchase a car. Instead, he used the money to improve his community. He bought an ambulance.

Gershom Sizomu has advocated for equal religious rights in Israel. So has . . .

Anat Hoffman

Israeli Civil & Religious Rights Activist, 1954–

When Anat was a child, her parents were proudly not religious. Living on a kibbutz outside Jerusalem, they had deep Jewish cultural identities, but ritual and prayer meant little or nothing to them. Like many secular Israelis, her parents considered "religious" to mean "rigidly Orthodox," and that lifestyle held no appeal to them. Anat absorbed her parents' values. She was driven, idealistic, and devoted to Israel, but not religiously inclined.

But then Anat left Israel to study in the United States. She no longer lived among Israelis and soon craved connection to other Jews. For the first time, she was exposed to more accepting, progressive forms of Judaism like Reform, Conservative, Reconstructionist, and a more liberal Orthodoxy. "I learned that there is more than one way to be a Jew," explains Anat.

In the United States, she immersed herself in synagogue life. When she returned to Israel, she was no longer secular. She called herself a *datiya reformit*—a Reform religious person.

Back in Jerusalem, Anat devoted herself to progressive causes and fighting the Orthodox Jewish establishment, which controls all official Jewish life in the country. She served 14 years on the Jerusalem City Council. She used her position to fight gender discrimination and advocate for equal pay for women and equal city services for Palestinians. For two decades, Anat led the Israel Religious Action Center, which advocates for equal religious rights for all Jews in Israel and civil rights for racial and ethnic minorities.

But Anat is perhaps best known for Women of the Wall, which she helped found in 1988 and now leads. The Orthodox authorities solely control access to the Western Wall in Jerusalem, the last remnant of the Second Temple and Judaism's holiest place. Women are not allowed to pray as a group, sing out loud or read Torah there. Once a month, Women of the Wall gathers at the Western Wall, challenging these laws. Protesters have spit at Anat, thrown bottles at her, and sworn at her, all in an effort to prevent her—and the Women of the Wall—from praying together. The police have arrested Anat numerous times for wearing a tallit or carrying a Torah scroll at the Western Wall. Anat, however, remains firm in her convictions. "We are fighting for a voice and a place at the holiest site," she says. "It's about who owns Judaism in Israel."

Anat Hoffman won medals in swimming at the Maccabiah Games. So did . . .

Mark Spitz

Olympic Swimming Champion, 1950–

Every day, Mark and his father went to Waikiki Beach near their home in Hawaii. Mark would run across the sand and jump into the water for his daily swim. At two years old, Mark already swam like a fish. His father could envision Mark as a champion. When he was six, Mark's family moved to California and Mark began swimming competitively. By age 10, Mark was breaking swimming records. Soon he was considered a swimming prodigy.

Mark's father pushed him hard, teaching, "Swimming isn't everything; winning is." Even Mark's bar mitzvah lessons were scheduled around his swimming workouts. When Mark was 14, the family moved so he could train at the famed Santa Clara Swim Club. With the move, Mark's father commuted more than 80 miles to work each day. The commute did not matter to him as long as Mark won races.

In 1965, 15-year-old Mark entered his first international competition—the Maccabiah Games in Tel Aviv. He won four gold medals and was named the Games' outstanding athlete. Three years later, Mark boastfully predicted that he would win six gold medals at the Mexico City Olympics. But he won *only* four medals—two gold, one silver and one bronze. He considered the Olympics to be a failure. "I just can't forget losing. I never will," says Mark.

In 1972, Mark went to the Olympic Games in Munich. Having learned his lesson, he made no predictions. Mark won each of his races in Munich. He won seven gold medals and set seven new records. For the next 36 years, Mark held the record for most gold medals won at a single Olympic Games.

The morning after Mark's seventh race, tragedy struck Munich's Olympic Village. Palestinian terrorists kidnapped and murdered 11 Israeli athletes. Immediately after the attack, American security guards formed a protective ring around Mark, afraid he might be targeted too, because he was Jewish. Mark was whisked out of Germany. "The memories of the Munich games for me are of triumph and tragedy," says Mark. "As the years rolled on, I . . . believe that it is the power of giving and participating in life that can make us overcome terrorism."

In 1985, Mark returned to Tel Aviv for the Maccabiah Games. At the opening ceremony, he lit the Maccabiah torch. Standing next to him were three children of Israeli Olympians murdered in Munich.

Mark Spitz won 11 Olympic medals during his career. Who won 10?

1972

Ágnes Keleti

Olympic Gymnast & Coach, 1921–

When Ágnes turned 99 years old, her doctor told her: "Stop doing splits on the floor!"

Ágnes reluctantly listened. Instead, she did her splits standing up, lifting her leg above her head. Ágnes knew far too well the importance of being flexible, both physically and mentally.

At age 16, Ágnes won her first of 10 Hungarian National Gymnastics Championships. She began training for the Olympics, but it took her another 15 years to become an Olympian. The 1940 and 1944 Olympics were cancelled because of World War II. But as a Jewish athlete, Ágnes faced even greater challenges.

Hungary, an ally of Nazi Germany, had passed a new law banning Jewish athletes from gymnasiums. One day, Ágnes arrived at the National Gymnastics Club and her coach pulled her aside. "I'm sorry, Ágnes. Everybody loves you here, but you can no longer train at the gym," said her coach.

Although stunned and angry, Ágnes refused to give up gymnastics. She trained secretly in a school basement until even that became unsafe. In 1944, the Nazis sent soldiers into Hungary. They began forcing Jewish men, women, and children into crowded train cars and taking them away to concentration camps.

Ágnes went into hiding. She purchased identity papers from a Christian girl, then escaped to a remote village where she found work as a maid. On her rare days off, Ágnes did gymnastics in an isolated field. Finally, World War II ended and Ágnes could train openly. She devoted herself to preparing for the Olympics. An injury prevented her from competing in the 1948 Olympics. Ágnes refused to give up and just trained harder.

In 1952, Ágnes finally competed in the Olympics. In Helsinki, Finland, she won four medals, including a gold. But she was not finished. Four years later, in Melbourne, Australia, Ágnes won six Olympic medals, including four gold. At 35 years old, she was the oldest gymnast ever to win gold.

After her victory in Melbourne, Ágnes made Aliyah to Israel. Over the next 50 years, she built Israel's gymnastics program. Ágnes felt at home in Israel. For the first time ever, she did not need to worry about antisemitism. She got married and had two sons. In her son Rafael's words: "For her, starting a family with kids and all that, that was her victory against the Nazis."

Ágnes Keleti first came to Israel because of the Maccabiah Games, founded by . . .

5
MACCA

Yosef Yekutieli

Founder of the Maccabiah Games, 1897–1982

Yosef loved everything about sports, especially soccer. He knew some people didn't think Jews could be athletes, especially in the Russian Empire where he was born. Yosef wanted to prove them wrong. Yosef moved to the land of Israel when he was twelve. He dedicated his life to making sports an important part of Israeli life.

In 1912, Yosef was thrilled when 20 Jewish athletes won medals at the Stockholm Olympics. But all of the athletes were European or American, not pioneers in the land of Israel like Yosef. He had an idea. Yosef lived in the new city of Tel Aviv. Maybe Tel Aviv could host an Olympic Games just for Jewish athletes.

Yosef told everybody about his idea. Most people laughed at him. They called his idea *meshuginah*, ridiculous. There wasn't a swimming pool, a running track or a stadium in Tel Aviv—or anywhere in the land of Israel, for that matter. How could the city host a Jewish Olympics?

Many years passed, and Yosef did many things: he was a soccer player, a soldier, a gym teacher, and a Zionist worker. He got married and had six children. Yet Yosef never forgot his dream of a Jewish Olympics. He still talked about it and, gradually, Yosef noticed that more and more people liked the idea.

In 1929, Yosef traveled to Europe and told an important gathering of Zionist leaders about a Jewish Olympics. The leaders didn't laugh at Yosef at all. Instead, they voted to hold the first Maccabiah Games in Tel Aviv. And they put Yosef in charge of planning it.

Back then, there were no computers or television. Many people didn't even have a telephone. Yosef recruited motorcyclists to ride thousands of miles, all the way to Europe, announcing the Maccabiah games along the way. These *Motosikiliztim* rode from Turkey to Poland to Germany to France to Belgium. Another caravan rode across Egypt to Greece then through Europe to London. Yosef rode with the second caravan. Jews everywhere greeted the *Motosikiliztim* with cheers.

In 1932, 390 athletes from 18 countries came to Tel Aviv for the First Maccabiah Games. A new stadium was built just for the games. The swimmers, however, swam in Haifa's harbor rather than a swimming pool.

Today, tens of thousands of Jewish athletes participate in Maccabiah Games each year. And it all began with a boy named Yosef who had a dream.

Yosef Yekutieli excelled at soccer. So did . . .

MACCABIAH
MARCH 6APRIL

Douglas Emhoff

Attorney & U.S. Second Gentleman, 1964–

Douglas was a typical Jewish kid. Well, he did wear a brown, fuzzy velour three-piece suit for his bar mitzvah (it was the 1970s). Like many of his friends, he went to Jewish summer camp and excelled at tennis and soccer. His mother says, like most Jewish mothers would proudly say, "My son is a wonderful guy, a wonderful son, and he's brilliant."

Douglas's family moved to California when he was 17. He went to college and law school. As he built up a successful practice in sports and entertainment law, he mingled with Olympic champions, football stars, and even creators of cartoon characters. His life was full.

Then he met Kamala Harris on a blind date in 2013. The morning after their first date, he emailed her with the message, "I really like you." They got married a year later. At the wedding, Kamala put a flower garland representing her Indian heritage around his neck and, following Jewish tradition, Douglas stomped on a glass. "Our relationship and the way I roll, my whole life has just been to support the people I love unequivocally, and they support me. The whole thing has been based on parity and mutual respect," says Douglas.

When Kamala announced her candidacy to become the vice president alongside Joe Biden, Douglas campaigned tirelessly for her. And when Joe and Kamala won, Douglas left his law firm—and all of its celebrity glamor—to avoid any conflict of interest. He made an important decision—not easy for some men—to allow his spouse's career to take precedence over his own. Of course, he is also the first man to be married to the Vice President of the United States. "It quickly became clear that this wasn't just about my love for my wife, but also about my love for this country," he writes. "Stepping back from my career as an entertainment lawyer was a decision that we made together—this was about something bigger than either of us."

Douglas does not shy away from politics. He is just not interested in the spotlight. Providing an example for other supportive men, Douglas says, "I'm not her [Kamala's] political adviser. I'm her husband. And so my role was to be there for her, to love her, to have her back, to talk it through, to help her."

Douglas Emhoff wore this designer's clothing to his wife's inauguration . . .

Ralph Lauren

Iconic Fashion Designer, 1939–

Lifshitz—Ralph never liked his last name. He wanted to portray a specific image—sophisticated, successful, and stylish. *Lifshitz* certainly didn't fit that mystique. Besides, kids mocked him for it. Ralph might be a yeshiva student and the Bronx-born son of a house painter from Belarus, but he had bigger dreams. So, at age 16, Ralph changed his last name to *Lauren*. That's how *Ralph Lauren* was born. Some people accuse Ralph of changing his name to hide his Jewish background. But Ralph answers, "Absolutely not. That's not what it's about."

Even though Ralph grew up in the 1960s, the age of bell bottoms and tie dye, he had a style all his own. He dressed in preppy clothing, inspired by classic movie stars like Fred Astaire and Cary Grant. "I had always loved the look of the old English gentleman who dressed in class and style. . . . That's the image I wanted. I loved fashion . . . but had no idea I could use that in terms of a career," says Ralph.

Ralph studied business for two years at Baruch College before dropping out. He preferred to learn on the job, not in school. After a brief stint in the Army, Ralph went to work at the fashion company Brooks Brothers. At age 28, Ralph launched the Ralph Lauren Company. His first product line was ties with a distinct, wide style. Ralph sold 1,200 ties to the luxury store Neiman Marcus. An order from Bloomingdale's followed. Soon, Ralph launched a men's clothing line, calling it Polo. "Well, what kind of people play polo?" he asks. "Wealthy, cosmopolitan, chic, wealthy. I wanted to create a concept for the name."

Over time, Ralph expanded into women's and children's clothing, housewares, and fragrances. Ralph opened a store in Beverly Hills on the famous Rodeo Drive, the first designer to have his own store. Today, there are Ralph Lauren stores throughout the world, including two in Israel. Ralph, a cancer survivor, donates generously to medical research. "I don't want to be remembered only for selling thousands of shirts," says Ralph.

Ralph strove to capture a country club culture prohibited to Jews of his generation. He created an image as much as he created clothing. "People ask how can a Jewish kid from the Bronx do preppy clothes?" Ralph says. "Does it have to do with class and money? It has to do with dreams."

Ralph Lauren has been photographed by . . .

CANTOR

Annie Leibovitz

Famed Portrait Photographer, 1949–

Annie grew up as a military kid. With their father in the Air Force, Annie and her five siblings moved around a lot: Connecticut, the Philippines, California, and Maryland. So, as a chronicle of her own childhood, Annie started to take photographs of all places where she lived—including selfies.

Annie went to the San Francisco Art Institute. She thought she might major in painting or arts education. But her first photography class convinced her to study photography. During college, Annie took time off to live on Kibbutz Amir in Israel, learning Hebrew and working on an archaeology dig. Photographs she took in Israel and at a San Francisco peace march of beat poet Allan Ginsberg helped Annie land a job at *Rolling Stone* magazine. After just two years, she was promoted to chief photographer at *Rolling Stone*.

At *Rolling Stone* and later *Vanity Fair*, Annie developed her specialty: intimate portraits of celebrities, including rock stars, politicians, actors, and athletes. Her subjects range from Queen Elizabeth II to Lady Gaga to LeBron James to the Obamas. In fact, she's photographed many of the heroes in this book, including Leonard Cohen, Bob Dylan, Gal Gadot, Natalie Portman, Daniel Radcliffe, Sheryl Sandberg, and, of course, herself. At first, Annie found photographing well-known people intimidating. But she grew into the role, becoming the most prominent celebrity photographer of her generation.

Annie heavily poses her portraits, using lots of light and bold colors. She likes to develop a rapport with her subjects to evoke emotion when photographing them. In addition to celebrity photography, Annie photographs her own family, chronicling her three children's childhoods and her life partner writer Susan Sontag's battle with cancer. Annie does not distinguish between family and professional photographs. "I don't have two lives," Leibovitz says. "This is one life, and the personal pictures and the assignment work are all part of it." Some family photographs capture Jewish moments, like her parents' renewal of their wedding vows and her father's funeral. She says, "I'm not a practicing Jew, but I feel very Jewish."

Annie sought advice from various mentors in her career, but when asked what advice she would give her younger self, Annie tellingly answered, "I don't think I could give advice to my younger self because she probably wouldn't listen."

Annie Leibowitz photographed . . .

CONTAX
Annie Leibovitz

Volodymyr Zelenskyy

President & Defender of Ukraine, 1978–

When Volodymyr was a teenager, factory fumes polluted Ukraine's air and gangs roamed the city of Kryyi Rih, where his family lived. Volodymyr refused to get pulled into the decay around him. He and his friends wore fancy suits to look different from the gangs. After high school, Volodymyr studied law. But instead of working as a lawyer when he graduated, he became a comedian, using humor to speak out against political corruption. He is best known for starring as the unlikely president of Ukraine in a television show entitled *Servant of the People*. Soon, though, he wanted to make a more direct impact. In a case of life imitating art, Volodymyr and his friends formed a real political party called Servant of the People. In 2019, Volodymyr won the Ukrainian presidency in a landslide, receiving 73% of the vote.

Volodymyr is Ukraine's first Jewish president. He tells the story of four brothers: "Three of them, their parents and their families became victims of the Holocaust. . . . The fourth brother survived. . . . Two years after the war, he had a son, and in 31 years, he had a grandson. In 40 more years, that grandson became president, and he is standing before you today."

As president, he has experienced very little antisemitism. But when first elected, he faced pressure from an unlikely source—the Jewish community. Some Ukrainian Jews worried that if Volodymyr was unsuccessful in office, it might lead to a revival of hate. Noting that Ukraine has the lowest level of antisemitism in Europe, Volodymyr said, "I have Jewish blood. And I'm president. Nobody cares."

Volodymr's presidency was forever altered when Russia invaded Ukraine in February 2022. Instantly, Volodymr became a wartime president, strategizing with the military and serving as a symbol of strength for Ukrainians and the world. Calmly but forcefully, Volodymr refused to leave Ukraine to govern in exile, earning respect, and admiration around the world.

Early in the invasion, Russia launched a missile strike that hit the Babi Yar Holocaust memorial in Kyiv. In response, Volodymr spoke directly to the Jewish community, "I am now addressing all the Jews of the world—can't you see what is happening? Therefore, it is very important that now millions of Jews around the world won't be silent. Nazism is born in silence. Therefore, shout about the killings of civilians. Shout about the killings of Ukrainians."

Volodymyr Zelenskyy resisted Russian pressure.
So did . . .

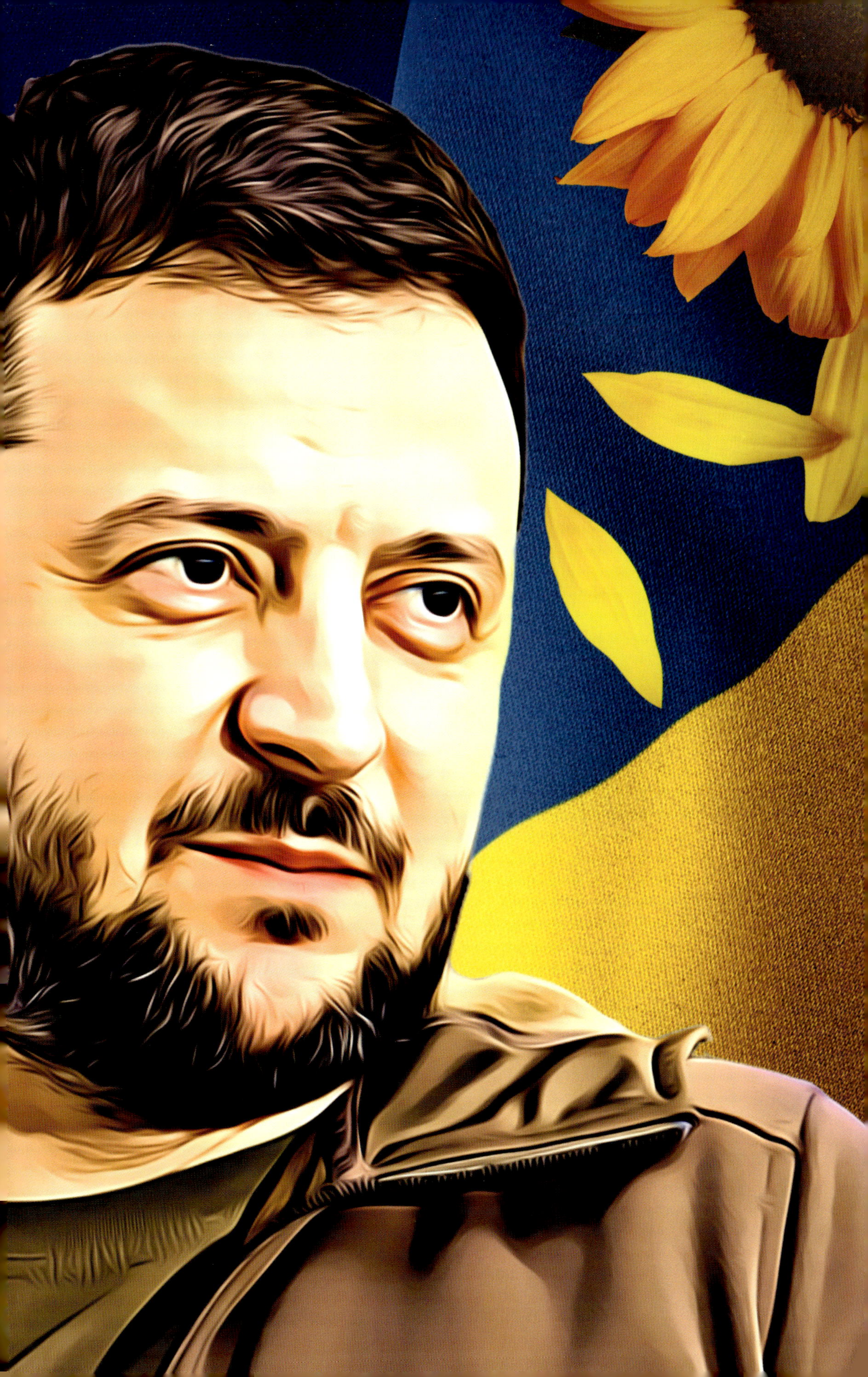

Avital Sharansky

Soviet Jewry Activist, 1950–

Sitting in a German airport lounge, Avital felt anticipation speeding the beating of her heart. She had not seen her husband Anatoly for 12 years. The day after their wedding, Avital left Moscow for Israel, but the Soviets did not allow Anatoly to join her. The newlyweds never imagined they would be separated for so long. In fact, when she left, Anatoly had said to her, "I'll see you soon in Jerusalem."

Finally, after all this time, they would be reunited. Avital saw an airport transport rush across the tarmac. Suddenly, Anatoly appeared in the lounge and pulled Avital into his arms. "I'm sorry that I'm late," he said.

Born in Ukraine, Avital only learned she was Jewish at age 14. Her parents kept it a secret for her own protection. The Soviets had outlawed Judaism. To help hide her heritage, her parents named her "Natalia," which means Christmas Day in Ukrainian. She changed her name to Avital in Israel.

As Avital grew into a young adult, she became more curious about Judaism. In Moscow, she secretly studied Hebrew and, in that class, met Anatoly. They attended their first Passover Seder together—a clandestine gathering at their Hebrew teacher's apartment. Bravely, they protested together at a Moscow synagogue during the 1973 Yom Kippur War.

As they fell in love, they made plans. Although it was risky, they applied for exit visas to move to Israel. The government approved Avital's application but rejected Anatoly's application. He became a "refusenik"—a Jewish person denied the right to leave the Soviet Union.

When she first arrived in Israel, Avital trusted that Anatoly would soon join her. But then the wait turned to horror. Anatoly was arrested, convicted of high treason, and sentenced to 13 years of hard labor in Siberia. Avital fought tirelessly for his release. Even though she was shy and quiet, she met with world leaders, spoke at rallies in front of thousands of people, and gave interviews on television. She and Anatoly became the face of the movement to free Soviet Jewry. "I am a private person," Avital says, "but I saw myself as a soldier."

When he arrived in Israel, Anatoly changed his name to Natan and became a political leader. Avital walked away from public life. She joyfully raised two daughters. Today, she is a grandmother. Her long journey to a loving, quiet life now complete, Avital says, "Through a sea of hatred, a sea of love. For me, it was just one long day that finally ended."

Avital Sharansky never planned on going into politics or having a public role. Neither did . . .

FREE
SOVIET
JEWS
אנטולי שרנסקי
ANATOLY SCHARANS
Solidarity Sunday
73

Claudia Sheinbaum Pardo

Former Mayor of Mexico City, 1962–

"Clau-di-a! Clau-di-a!" People shouted the name of the newly elected mayor of Mexico City. Claudia felt like a celebrity. Only a few years before that moment in 2018, she had been a quiet environmental researcher with little interest in politics.

Claudia's parents met as leftist activists in college and raised Claudia and her siblings to value making their voices heard. She remembers a childhood rich with political discussion. Professionally, both of Claudia's parents are scientists. Her mother especially inspired Claudia to become a scientist. Claudia's parents are devoutly secular, but Claudia has strong memories of celebrating Jewish holidays with her immigrant grandparents.

Claudia majored in physics in college, then earned a PhD in environmental engineering. Mexico City is a congested, densely populated metropolis of 24 million people. Claudia researched the relationship in Mexico City between transportation, energy, and climate change. Like her parents, she was a student activist. She helped form the Revolutionary Democratic Party, an influential leftist opposition party in Mexico. Andrés Manuel López Obrador, Mexico City's mayor, appointed her as the city's Secretary of the Environment in 2000. With this position, she also joined a United Nations panel on climate change that received the Nobel Peace Prize in 2007.

With Andrés Manuel López Obrador as her mentor, she was elected mayor of Mexico City's Tlalpan district in 2015. When Andrés became Mexico's president, Claudia campaigned to replace him as Mexico City's mayor. In 2018, Claudia beat six other candidates and became the city's first female and first Jewish mayor.

As mayor, Claudia developed a six-year environmental plan aimed at reducing air pollution by 30%, planting 15 million trees, and increasing recycling, public transportation, and solar power. Claudia sees science as a perfect preparation for politics. "Training in physics makes you always look for the root causes. Why is something happening? That's fundamental for politics," says Claudia. "And then engineering is much more focused on the 'how.' How can I solve it?"

Being mayor of Mexico City is seen as a steppingstone to the country's presidency. Indeed, in September 2023, Claudia was nominated as Mexico's ruling party's candidate for president. If elected, she'll be Mexico's first Jewish and first female president."

Claudia Sheinbaum Pardo is an expert on engineering and the environment. So was . . .

Simcha Blass

Israeli Inventor of Drip Irrigation, 1897–1982

Growing up in Warsaw, Poland, Simcha dreamt of living in the land of Israel. From a religiously observant family, Simcha studied traditional Jewish texts but also developed a keen interest in engineering. While studying at a technical college and later serving in the Polish army, Simcha invented many useful items—a device to measure wind direction, a machine to assist in planting wheat, and other creations. With all his inventions, Simcha returned to a single question: How could any of it be used in the land of Israel?

Finally, in the 1920s, Simcha left Poland behind. He immigrated to Kibbutz Degania Bet near the Sea of Galilee. Simcha quickly realized the importance of water in the Yishuv, the name for the Jewish community in British Mandate Palestine. He turned his inventor's mind to optimizing water resources and soon became the chief water engineer for the Yishuv. He planned the first modern aqueduct, a system of canals and pipes to carry water throughout the land of Israel. The Negev desert proved especially challenging. In 1946, Simcha imported British water pipes leftover from fighting fires during World War II. Simcha and his crew laid the pipes to provide water to Arab Bedouins and 11 new Jewish communities in the Negev.

But Simcha's most important invention happened nearly by accident. When visiting one of the Negev settlements, Simcha noticed something odd. He saw one lush tree surrounded by several struggling ones. Stooping under the lush tree, Simcha began to dig and discovered a small leak in a water pipe running under the tree. These few escaping drops were enough to allow the tree to thrive.

Based on his discovery, Simcha developed a system for placing dripping hoses close to the ground in order to nurture agriculture—especially in the desert. Drip irrigation allowed the deserts of Israel to bloom with crops. But Simcha wasn't finished. He founded a company called Netafim, which means "drops of water," to bring drip irrigation to the rest of the world. Today, over 100 countries use systems made by Netafim.

Simcha's discovery made agriculture viable in the driest deserts and helps feed people worldwide, especially in developing countries. And it all started with a young boy who had an inventive spirit and dreams of the land of Israel.

Simcha Blass liked to tinker and invent. So did . . .

Hedy Lamarr

Actor, Model & Inventor, 1914–2000

By her 10th birthday, Hedy could speak four languages, play piano beautifully, and dance like a pro. Born into a wealthy family with Jewish roots in Vienna, Austria, Hedy attended only the most elite schools. Known for her stunning looks, Hedy signed her first modeling contract at age 12. Her parents and the household servants nicknamed her "Princess Hedy."

Hedy had one simple pleasure: taking long walks with her father through the Wienerwald, the forest near their home. On these walks, her father told her all about technology. He described machines like printing presses and streetcars, how they worked, and how they helped society. What could she invent to make the world a better place?

Hedy grew more beautiful with each passing year. By age 18, she was starring in movies. But Hedy wanted to be known for more than her looks. She said, "Any girl can be glamorous. All you have to do is stand still and look stupid."

Louis B. Mayer, head of MGM studios, "discovered" Hedy and brought her to California. He touted her as the "most beautiful woman in the world." Hedy quickly became a glamorous Hollywood star, appearing in many movies. In her free time, she worked on her inventions. She even set up a workshop on movie sets so she could tinker with electronics between filming takes.

In 1940, at the height of her Hollywood career, Hedy heard a devastating news report. A Nazi submarine torpedoed a cruise ship that was evacuating 90 schoolchildren from war-torn Great Britain to Canada. Seventy-seven of the children drowned. Hedy was outraged. Could technology prevent similar catastrophes in the future? Hedy went to work. She developed a sonar system to locate submarines. The Allies adapted her sonar system to prevent future attacks. Her invention contributed to the development of modern Wi-Fi, cellphone, and Bluetooth technology.

After retiring from movies, Hedy avoided publicity and became something of a recluse. But she kept on inventing. She created a new kind of traffic light, advancements to jet engines, and a skin-tightening technique based on the way an accordion works. During her life, Hedy was celebrated more for her looks than her brains. But after her death, she received recognition as an inventor and was even inducted into the National Inventors Hall of Fame.

A mini-series about Hedy Lamarr stars . . .

UNITED STATES PATENT
Hedy Kiesler
Aug. 11, 1942.

Gal Gadot

Actor & Feminist, 1985–

While in high school, Gal started getting offers for modeling contracts. Not wanting to make money from her looks, she worked at Burger King instead. Gal's parents had taught her and her sister "to believe that we're capable, to value ourselves." Growing up in Israel, Gal played basketball, volleyball, and tennis. She studied dance for 12 years. She says, "There was no TV-watching. It was always 'Take a ball and go play.'"

After high school graduation, Gal had two months off before her Israeli army duty began. To fill that gap, Gal's mother and best friend entered her in the Miss Israel pageant. Gal was stunned when she won. Although being Miss Israel gave Gal new opportunities, she quickly grew tired of it. When she competed in the Miss Universe pageant, she purposely broke rules that she found silly—like wearing evening gowns to breakfast. She wasn't surprised or unhappy when she didn't win.

Instead of being Miss Universe, Gal served in the Israel Defense Forces (IDF). She did so well in basic training that the army made her a combat instructor. "I wish no country had the need for an army. But in Israel serving is part of being an Israeli. You've got to give back to the state," says Gal.

After the army, Gal studied law. She only lasted one year in college before a Hollywood agent recruited her to audition. She landed a part in the action movie *Fast and Furious*, in which she did all her own stunts. *Wonder Woman* came next. "When I saw myself in the mirror wearing the *Wonder Woman* costume for the first time, I was like, 'Oh my God!' Who would have thought . . . Gal, from this tiny part of the world, would be here in this room in the States in *this* role?"

Just as *Wonder Woman* descended from strong Amazon women, Gal's family history molded her. Her father's family has lived in Israel for six generations. On her mother's side, her grandparents survived the Holocaust. Gal traveled to Poland with her high school. She says, "I returned home more mature and cried with my grandfather about that, coming a full circle from his childhood to mine."

The circling of generations continues. These days, Gal is raising her three daughters to be Wonder Women—strong, self-assured, and proud.

Gal Gadot was crowned Miss Israel. So was . . .

סבבה!
(COOL!)

Yityish "Titi" Aynaw

Israeli Beauty Queen from Ethiopia, 1991–

Titi was born in the Jewish village of Chahawit in Ethiopia. Her family lived in a one-room home with no electricity or running water. Life was hard and Titi experienced a lot of loss. Her father died when she was a baby; her mother died when she was 12. Like so many other Ethiopian Jews, her grandparents had emigrated to Israel years before. Orphaned, Titi and her brother left Ethiopia to join them. Until then, everything Titi knew about Israel came from the Bible. "I was surprised by what I saw in Israel—buildings, cars, industrialization," she says.

Titi went to a boarding school in Haifa. "They threw me into the deep water. But that's how you learn to swim the best," says Titi. Her determination paid off. In high school, she was elected student council president, excelled in track and field, and won a national film competition. In the army, Titi rose to the rank of lieutenant. Given the choice of commanding a unit of 300 men or women, Titi chose the men. She thought that working with the men would be a bigger challenge and an opportunity to prove herself.

Encouraged by her best friend, Titi entered the Miss Israel contest in 2013. When the judges asked why she deserved the title, Titi said it was about time that a Black woman wore the crown. She won—the first Miss Israel of African descent. Quickly, Titi became an internet sensation, and her picture graced the covers of Israeli magazines. As Miss Israel, Titi now had a platform to advocate for other Ethiopian Jews. She also had new opportunities, like dining with President Barack Obama.

When Titi first immigrated to Israel, her classmates taught her a few Hebrew words each day. They called it "Project Titi." Paying it forward, Titi founded an education center for at-risk children. She calls it "Titi's Project." Titi says, "I know racism and tokenism exist in Israel. I'm not here to complain about it, I'm here to change it."

Titi's full name, Yityish, means "look" in Amharic, like "looking toward the future." She explains, "I was born sick, but my mom believed I had a future." Many Ethiopian Jews adopted Hebrew names when they settled in Israel. Not Titi. "I'd never change my name. Ever."

Titi looked forward and saw herself as a role model.

Titi Aynaw was born in Ethiopia. So was . . .

Ababa
Harer
ETHIOPIA

Naomi Wadler

Student Activist for Gun Control, 2006–

It was going to be a big day for Naomi and her family. They argued about what she would wear. Naomi wanted to wear something casual and all black. Her mom wanted her to wear a dress and something more colorful. Naomi stood her ground but accepted her aunt's compromise. Her aunt quickly knit a bright orange scarf—which has since become iconic for Naomi—a symbol of gun violence awareness.

Wearing that scarf, Naomi, only 11 years old at the time, spoke before 800,000 people at the 2018 pro-gun control protest March For Our Lives in Washington, DC. She had never given a public speech before. She was the youngest speaker at the march. She felt terrified and sang in the car on the way over to calm her nerves. But afterward, she felt very good. Naomi highlighted in her message that females are most notably the victims of gun violence. She said, "I represent the African American women who are victims of gun violence, who are simply statistics instead of vibrant, beautiful girls full of potential."

Naomi was adopted from an Ethiopian orphanage. Naomi says, "I am Black. I am an immigrant. I am a Jew. I have an opinion. And I am not going anyplace. Get used to it."

Naomi began her activism when she organized a walkout with her classmates at her elementary school following the 2018 shooting at the Marjory Stoneman Douglas High School in Parkland, Florida. The daughter of Naomi's mom's best friend was killed during the shooting. This motivated Naomi to get involved. She also wanted to call attention to the murder of Courtlin Arrington, a Black girl in Birmingham, Alabama, who was shot and killed by her boyfriend in school, but whose death received little media attention.

Since the March For Our Lives, Naomi has celebrated her bat mitzvah. She has also spoken at the Women in the World Annual Summit and the *Teen Vogue* summit. At the Tribeca Film Festival, she received the Disruptive Innovation Award. In her free time, she plays tennis and watches television to unwind.

Looking ahead, Naomi plans to continue with her activism. She says, "Black women [are] really what I like to focus on because we're not really seen as women. We're seen as things. I love treating people like people."

Naomi Walder spoke at the March for our Lives, an event sponsored and attended by . . .

Steven Spielberg

Renowned Director, Producer & Screenwriter, 1946–

As a young boy, Steven was a C student and the butt of bullies' jokes. Steven's family moved a lot: from Ohio to New Jersey, Arizona, and eventually California. Steven grew up Orthodox but felt ashamed of his Jewish identity. "I was embarrassed, I was self-conscious, I was always aware I stood out because of my Jewishness," says Steven.

Still, Steven had a creative mind and supportive parents. He says, "I consider my mom my lucky charm. And when I was 12 years old, my father handed me a movie camera, the tool that allowed me to make sense of this world." With that camera, Steven made his first movie, earning a merit badge in Boy Scouts. Next, he made a 40-minute film entitled *Escape to Nowhere*, which won a statewide competition. At age 16, he made his first full-length feature film. It had a $500 budget, underwritten by his father, and played at a local theater for one evening.

Steven applied to study film at the University of Southern California but was rejected. So he enrolled at California State University Long Beach. He dropped out during his sophomore year, when he landed his dream job at Universal Studios. Steven's big break came in 1975 when he directed the blockbuster *Jaws*. *Indiana Jones*, *E.T.*, *Jurassic Park*, and many other films followed. Along the way, he won three Academy Awards and scores of other honors.

In 1982, Steven gained the rights to make a movie about Oskar Schindler, a German factory owner who saved 1,200 Jews during the Holocaust. Steven's father lost many relatives in the Holocaust, so the movie had deep importance to Steven. Yet he put off working on *Schindler's List* for a decade. "I had a fear of doing *Schindler's List* that made me delay it year after year. I wasn't old enough to make this movie in 1982. I had to have a family first. I had to figure out what my place was in the world," says Steven. With profits from *Schindler's List*, Steven established the Righteous Persons Foundation. Steven says, "I had been so ashamed of being a Jew and now I'm filled with pride." Steven's 2022 film, *The Fabelmans*, is based on his years as an adolescent and his first years as a filmmaker.

Remember how Steven dropped out of college? Thirty-something years later, he re-enrolled and graduated. He wanted to be a role model for his children. Cal State did help him out—they gave him three credits in paleontology for *Jurassic Park*.

Steven Spielberg's Schindler's List
features music played by . . .

Itzhak Perlman

Virtuoso on Violin, 1945–

In their Tel Aviv apartment, Itzhak's mother tuned the kitchen radio to a station playing classical music. Itzhak, just two years old, began to hum along, making the sounds of the different instruments in the orchestra. Itzhak's mother smiled and thought to herself, "Perhaps Itzhak will be musical." When a violin solo began, little Itzhak hummed even louder. Violins were his favorite.

When Itzhak was three years old, two important things happened. Israel became a nation and Itzhak got his first violin. By age six, he was performing with an orchestra. When Itzhak was 13, a talent scout from the *Ed Sullivan Show* heard him play and brought him to the U.S. to perform on television. Itzhak and his family moved to New York so he could enroll in the Juilliard School of Music. Today, Itzhak is considered perhaps the world's greatest violinist. He has played with every major orchestra in the world and has won 16 Grammy awards.

Itzhak has done all this without the full use of his legs. When Itzhak was four, he contracted polio, which paralyzed his legs. He walks with braces and crutches or uses a scooter. Since solo violinists traditionally stand when playing, Itzhak worried his paralysis might hold him back. But it hasn't. He just plays sitting down. Concert halls with stairs are bothersome, but Itzhak isn't deterred. Both by being a role model and an advocate, Itzhak promotes greater accessibility in public places for people with disabilities. Itzhak says, "I can't walk very well, but I'm not onstage to do walking. I'm on the stage to play."

As a teenager, Itzhak met a violin student named Toby Friedlander. The first time Toby heard Itzhak play, she jokingly asked him to marry her. Years later, Itzhak and Toby did marry; they had five children. Judaism is a driving force in Itzhak's life. He and Toby keep a kosher home and he does not perform on Shabbat. As a child, Itzhak dreamt of playing with the Israeli Philharmonic Orchestra. Itzhak has fulfilled that dream many times over. In 2016, Itzhak received the Genesis Prize, dubbed the "Jewish Nobel Prize," for his musical contributions and disability advocacy.

Decades have passed since Itzhak was a toddler, mimicking the violin he heard on the radio. But music still fills him with wonder. He says, "I am constantly stimulated and amazed by the music and the different ways of interpreting it. The work keeps me young."

To help preserve Yiddish musical traditions, Itzhak Perlman has worked closely with . . .

Aaron Lansky

Founder of the Yiddish Book Center, 1955-

Asleep in his Massachusetts apartment, Aaron got an emergency phone call in the middle of the night. Thousands of Yiddish books were sitting in a Brooklyn, New York, dumpster and would go to the landfill in the morning. Aaron rushed to the train station to get to Brooklyn. He had a mission: save Yiddish books.

During his childhood, Aaron Lansky's mother and grandmother spoke Yiddish when they didn't want Aaron and his two brothers to understand them. Yiddish, a combination of mostly German and Hebrew, was their "secret language." Jewish immigrants from Eastern Europe spoke it, but Aaron's generation did not.

In college, Aaron took a course on the Holocaust. During that course, Aaron became fascinated by Jewish culture that the Nazis destroyed, including Yiddish. Yiddish was a dying language. By the time Aaron started graduate school to focus on East European Jewish studies, Aaron had trouble finding books in Yiddish in the school library or bookstore. He then realized he was looking in the wrong place. He learned that young people often threw Yiddish books away. They had inherited the books but couldn't read the language, so the books didn't seem to serve a purpose.

Aaron considered these books precious, the Jewish people's "portable homeland." He announced that he would collect any Yiddish books that people wanted to donate. "People wrote back and said things like, 'For 40 years I have had these books because someday I knew they would be important. Now you can come and take them from me,'" recollects Aaron.

He drove from place to place to collect any Yiddish books that he heard about or that someone wrote or called to tell him about. When Aaron began his quest, scholars estimated that 70,000 Yiddish books remained in the world–but Aaron eventually collected 1.5 million books from around the world, including Cuba, Russia, and Congo.

These days, 40 people work at the Yiddish Book Center in Amherst, Massachusetts. The center has digitized and translated many books, and it organizes educational programs for students of all ages. It has distributed books to 600 research libraries in 26 countries. Aaron says, "It started out as an attempt to save books that were being destroyed and has become an organization capable of making real changes in American Jewish life."

The boy Aaron cracked the code. He learned his mother and grandmother's secret language and shared it with the world.

Aaron Lansky's Yiddish Book Center produced a documentary about . . .

THE TREMENDOUS SUCCESS OF THE PEOPLES THEATRE
יענקי-דודל
דער אידישער
THE JEWISH YANKEE DOODLE
1. COMPANY.
2. BUSINESS BEFORE PLEASURE
BY
ARR. BY
J. KAMENETZKY
PUBLISHED BY
THEODORE LOHR
GREAT MUSICAL PRODUCTION
GOLEM
in 3 Acts and Prologue
Lyrics By SHARGEL FRIEDSEL

Leonard Nimoy

Actor, Best Known as Star Trek's Spock, 1931–2015

On Yom Kippur, Leonard sat between his father and his older brother, Melvin, in their Boston synagogue. The services were long, but Leonard didn't mind. When else could he spend the whole day with his father? Usually, his father, an immigrant from Ukraine, worked long hours as a barber. When Leonard was not in school, he had a newspaper route and shined shoes to help support his family. Today, though, he could just enjoy sitting with his father and brother.

Leonard's favorite part of the service was the priestly benediction. It was theatrical and haunting. The rabbi and cantor called the synagogue elders in front of the ark. The elders covered their heads with their *tallitot* (prayer shawls), raised their hands, and spread their fingers into the Hebrew letter *shin*. Then they chanted in Hebrew. Leonard was mesmerized. Years later, he said, "I had no idea what was going on, but the sound of it and the look of it was magical."

Leonard had a good voice and sang in the synagogue choir. His own bar mitzvah went so well that he sang again the following week for another boy's bar mitzvah. After high school, Leonard's parents wanted him to go to college and pursue a "practical" career. But Leonard's grandfather encouraged him to pursue what he loved: acting.

For over a decade, Leonard acted in bit roles. He enlisted in the army and was assigned to a unit of entertainers that put on shows for other troops. In 1965, finally, Leonard's big break came. In *Star Trek*'s television pilot, Leonard was cast as Spock, half-human, half-Vulcan (a highly logical, non-human species). He played Spock for nearly 50 years, including three television seasons and in eight feature films. Since Leonard played Spock for so long, some say it affected his own personality, making him more analytical and remote. His connection to Spock was deep but conflicted. Leonard published two autobiographies: *I Am Not Spock* in 1975 and *I Am Spock* in 1995.

When he first started playing Spock, Leonard wanted to create a Vulcan hand salute. He remembered Yom Kippur as a boy and the magical feeling of seeing the priestly benediction. Leonard lifted his hands and spread his fingers into the Hebrew letter *shin*. But just the hand motion was not enough. A greeting needs a catch phrase. Like all good Vulcans, Leonard called out, "Live long and prosper."

Leonard Nimoy appeared on Big Bang Theory, a show that starred . . .

Mayim Bialik

Actor, Writer & Neuroscientist, 1975–

"As a kid, I felt really weird," says Mayim. "I'm definitely on the spectrum of socially awkward." Growing up in San Diego, California, Mayim read comics and science fiction. She played multiple instruments and acted in school plays. At age 12, Mayim was cast in the movie *Pumpkinhead*. From there, Mayim landed the lead in the popular sitcom *Blossom*.

When *Blossom* ended after five seasons, Mayim chose college over acting. "Three of my four grandparents are immigrants to this country, so I grew up with a very strong ethic to go to college, no matter what, even if you had your own television show, you had to go to college." Accepted to Yale and Harvard, Mayim instead chose UCLA and majored in neurobiology and Judaic studies. She went on to earn a doctorate in neurobiology. By the time she finished graduate school, Mayim was married with two sons. She didn't think being a research scientist allowed enough family time, so she turned back to acting.

Mayim was cast as Dr. Amy Farrah Fowler on the sitcom *Big Bang Theory*—a fitting role since Dr. Fowler, like Mayim, is a neuroscientist. Originally meant to be a supporting character, Dr. Fowler's role quickly grew and Mayim became one of the show's stars. "I've never been driven by money, by fame, that's not really my shtick. I'm a performer. I've been a performer my whole life and I love entertaining people. That being said, being in a more prominent position publicly has allowed me to expand the scope of my Jewish presence, and that's been very personally gratifying," says Mayim.

Mayim grew up Reform and now follows Orthodoxy, including almost always wearing skirts. She considers this choice feminist: "That really is the ultimate aspect of Orthodox feminism—feeling empowered by the way you dress in a way that makes you feel confident and good about yourself."

She is a proud Zionist and has faced backlash for standing up for Israel. "Israel deserves to live as an autonomous free and safe nation. The Palestinian people deserve the same. What is happening now by extremists on both sides is tragic," says Mayim.

A mother, actor, and Jewish activist, Mayim estimates she sleeps about four hours a night. She says, "Every day is lined up right next to the other one for a reason. The best you can do is do each day well with kindness and as a good person."

Mayim Bialik grew up reading books by . . .

Judy Blume

Groundbreaking Novelist for Kids & Teens, 1938-

Growing up in Elizabeth, New Jersey, Judy was always creating stories in her head. Every afternoon before dinner, she bounced a ball against the wall of her house, sometimes for hours on end, thinking up new stories. It was her special time to be alone and, because of her imagination, she never felt lonely. Judy didn't tell anybody about her imaginative world; she didn't want to seem different.

Judy's childhood was not easy. Judy's father had six brothers and sisters; nearly all of them died while she was a child. She says, "A lot of my philosophy came from growing up in a family that was always sitting shiva." When her brother fell seriously ill, Judy, her brother, and her mother went to Florida for a year so he could recuperate. Her father stayed in New Jersey to work. Judy worried constantly that something would happen to him while they were away.

Judy got married while she was still a student at New York University. Not long after graduation, she had a daughter, then a son. A stay-at-home mom, Judy began writing to satisfy her creative side. For two and a half years, she sent stories to publishers and got nothing but rejection letters. But Judy stuck with it. Finally, in 1969, a publisher accepted her picture book *The One in the Middle is the Green Kangaroo.*

The next year, Judy published *Are You There God? It's Me, Margaret,* a book about an eleven-year-old girl with questions about faith and her changing body. Until then, books for pre-teens and teens did not talk about sexuality, spirituality, and puberty—at least, not with such honesty. "I think I write about sexuality because it was uppermost in my mind when I was a kid: the need to know, and not knowing how to find out," says Judy. The book established Judy as a premier author for children and teens. Judy wrote many more books, including *Tales of a Fourth Grade Nothing, Blubber,* and *Deenie.*

Not everybody approved of Judy's honest approach. Her books routinely appear on banned book lists. But her fans far outnumber her critics. Over 90 million copies of her books have sold worldwide. They have been translated into 32 languages and been made into movies. And it all began with a quiet girl with a lot of imagination.

Judy Blume graduated from New York University.
So did . . .

Idina Menzel

Singer & Actor called "Queen of Broadway", 1971-

Eleven-year-old Idina ran with her bunkmates through the dark. They had a goal: getting to the boys' cabins. "We got scared, we screamed, we got caught," she said. "But we made it over to say hello to the boys!" Determined and driven, Idina usually meets her goals.

Idina says camp was "invaluable" to her. It helped her build her leadership skills and her self-esteem. She formed lifelong friendships at camp and she got her theatrical start there. The summer that she successfully snuck to the boys' cabins, she also appeared in the camp production of *Oliver* and loved it. Soon, singing and acting became Idina's passion. Her grandfather bought Idina her first piano. Her father arranged for singing lessons.

As a teenager, theater kept her going through difficult times. On Thanksgiving Day when Idina was 15, her parents told her that they planned to divorce. "There were tough times in my teenage years when my parents divorced and the holidays became a little more complicated," says Idina.

To support her mother and herself and pay for her education at New York University, Idina sang at weddings and b'nai mitzvah parties. But Idina had a goal: making it on Broadway. Determined as always, Idina worked hard and did not give up. Her first Broadway role was in the musical *Rent*. Then she played Elphaba Thropp, the Wicked Witch of the West, in *Wicked*—a role that truly captured the hearts of theatergoers, particularly young girls. Her fame grew to global proportions when she voiced Elsa in the animated film *Frozen*, singing the Oscar-winning song "Let it Go." "I love that I play all of these strong women—they have a deep vulnerability and need to go through a journey to harness their power," says Idina.

Idina credits "hard work, discipline, practice and surrounding myself with people who are honest with me" for her success. To give back to the next generation, Idina created a sleepaway theater camp for girls from underprivileged households. Over the summer, she works with the girls to help them develop their talent as budding singers and actors.

Speaking to her young fans, Idina says, "You can't get it all right all the time, but you can try your best. If you've done that, all that's left is to accept your shortcomings and have the courage to try to overcome them." In other words, *let it go*.

Idina Menzel graduated from Syosset High School on Long Island, New York. So did . . .

Natalie Portman

Award-winning Actor & Activist, 1981–

Natalie faced a dilemma. Most aspiring actors only dream of a role in a *Star Wars* movie. Natalie, at age 16, had been cast as Queen Amidala in *Stars Wars: Episode I*. After months of filming and editing, Natalie looked forward to the movie premiere and walking down the red carpet. But that night, she also needed to study for her high school final exams. Natalie made her choice: she stayed home and studied. In the fall, Natalie headed off to Harvard. "I don't care if [college] ruins my career. . . . I'd rather be smart than a movie star," said Natalie.

Born in Jerusalem, Natalie and her family immigrated to the United States when she was three years old. They lived in Maryland and Connecticut before settling on Long Island, New York. Natalie attended Jewish day school, loved dance, and dreamed of becoming an astronaut. Like many hopeful actors, Natalie changed her last name. Instead of Hershlag, she chose Portman, her grandmother's family name.

Natalie landed her first movie role at age 14. Other roles followed, including playing Anne Frank on Broadway. She found this role especially difficult, because her grandparents lost family in the Holocaust. "Anne Frank's faith in humanity, even when she was starving and sick, had a huge impact on me," said Natalie. She won an Academy Award for playing a troubled ballerina in *Black Swan*. By then, Natalie had a psychology degree from Harvard. It helped her prepare for her role.

She has the reputation of being a precise actor, who shows emotion through the smallest details like a teardrop or a nod of her head. Many of Natalie's films have Jewish themes. She wrote and directed her first feature, *A Tale of Love and Darkness*, based on the memoir of the famous Israeli author Amos Oz.

Whether on screen or in her personal life, Natalie lives her principles. She's been a vegan since age nine and doesn't wear leather. She is outspoken about causes like women's empowerment and promoting peace in Israel. She says that her relationship with Israel is "very complicated, like family—you love it more than anything else in the world and you also are more critical of it than anything else in the world."

Natalie built a name for herself acting "in a galaxy far, far away." But she says, "There's such a big world beyond acting and beyond films."

Natalie Portman is fluent in six languages.
Who was fluent in ten?

Moe Berg

Baseball Catcher, Linguist & Spy, 1902-1972

Moe was just an average baseball player, a third-string catcher traded between the White Sox, Red Sox, Indians, Dodgers, and Washington Senators for 15 seasons. He only had one hit the entire 1931 season. But strangely, in 1934, Moe was chosen for the Major League All-Star Team. He even traveled to Japan for an exposition game with baseball greats like Babe Ruth and Lou Gehrig. Why?

It was a secret at the time, but Moe wasn't just a baseball catcher—he was also a spy. While in Japan with the All-Stars, Moe snuck up the tallest building in Tokyo to film the Tokyo skyline, harbor, and weapons factories. During World War II, the U.S. military used Moe's movies to plan air raids.

Legendary manager Casey Stengel called Moe "the strangest man ever to play baseball."

He may also have been among the smartest. Moe spoke ten languages. According to popular legend, Moe taught himself Japanese on the boat ride to Asia. In the dugout during each game, he would read as many as a dozen newspapers. Confirming his reputation as a "brainiac," Moe appeared three times on the radio quiz show *Information, Please*. A graduate of Princeton University, Moe got a law degree from Columbia University while also playing in the Major League. He did skip spring training sometimes to study.

From childhood, Moe enjoyed being a mystery. He joined his first baseball team at age seven in his hometown of Newark, New Jersey. Moe's father, an immigrant from Russia, didn't approve of baseball, calling it a distraction from school. Whether to keep a secret from his father or just for fun, young Moe signed up for the team under the pseudonym "Runt Wolfe." Later in life, Moe's spy name was "Remus," after a character in Roman mythology who was raised by a wolf.

In 1942, Moe joined the agency that would become the CIA. Hiding the fact that he was Jewish, Moe traveled deep into Europe to learn about the Nazi nuclear program. Before he went, he learned physics with tutoring help from Albert Einstein. After World War II, Moe continued as a spy with missions into the Soviet Union.

Unfortunately, Moe died before he could write his autobiography. Many of Moe's secrets as baseball player-turned-spy died with him. Then again, perhaps Moe preferred it that way.

Moe Berg played for the Dodgers. So did . . .

MORRIS (MOE) BERG
MORRIS
MOE) BERG
MORRIS
MOE) BERG
MORRIS
MOE) BERG
MORRIS
MOE) BERG
MORRIS
MOE) BERG

Sandy Koufax

All-Star Baseball Pitcher, 1935–

Sandy grew up in Brooklyn in a loving, supportive, blended family. When Sandy was three, his parents divorced. His mother remarried and his stepfather doted on him, taking him to the Yiddish theater and encouraging his interest in sports. In his high school yearbook, Sandy included his life goal: "To be successful and make my family proud of me."

By high school, Sandy was over six feet tall and a natural on the basketball court. The University of Cincinnati recruited him with a basketball scholarship. He was simply a "walk-on" for the baseball team. But during his freshman year, a baseball scout saw Sandy—who was left-handed—pitch. The scout was so impressed that he signed Sandy with the Brooklyn Dodgers. Sandy got a $14,000 signing bonus. He figured that if baseball didn't work out, he could use the money to finish college.

Sandy had a slow start with the Dodgers. For his first several years, Sandy could not control his throw—it was fast and wild. After a disappointing season in 1960, Sandy knew he might be sent down to the minor league. He considered giving up baseball. But another Jewish teammate, a catcher named Norm Sherry, pulled Sandy aside and gave him some advice. He told Sandy to slow his pitches down to gain more control. Following Norm's guidance, Sandy transformed his pitching. Sandy pitched a total of 12 seasons for the Dodgers. He was an all-star seven times and a World Series champion four times. In 1972, he was elected to the Baseball Hall of Fame—the youngest inductee ever. Today, he is considered one of the best pitchers in baseball history.

In the Jewish community, Sandy is best known for his integrity and convictions, not his athletic skill. In 1965, at the height of Sandy's career, the Dodgers made it to the World Series. Sandy knew his team needed him to help win the championship. But the first game of the series fell on Yom Kippur, the holiest day on the Jewish calendar. Sandy wasn't especially religious, but he sat the game out. Sandy knew his fans were watching. He felt some things were more important than baseball. "I'm Jewish. I'm a role model. I want them to understand they have to have pride," said Sandy.

"Pulling a Koufax" became an expression meaning to do the right thing. By not playing on Yom Kippur, Sandy Koufax became a symbol of Jewish pride.

Sandy Koufax chose not to work on a religious holiday. Who advocates for teachers to have that same right?

Baseball
Koufax
World
Koufax, Dodg

Randi Weingarten

Labor Leader & Attorney, 1957–

When Randi was in 11th grade, two events happened that propelled her toward a future as a labor organizer, fighting for workers' rights. First, Randi's mother, an elementary school teacher in Rockland County, New York, went on strike with her union to demand higher pay and smaller classes. For seven weeks, Randi walked the picket line with her mother. While on strike, her mother didn't earn a salary. As Randi's family struggled to pay their bills during the strike, she understood the teachers' strong commitment to get better working conditions.

That same year, the school board cut $2 million from the district budget. The cuts would have ended programs like driver's education. Randi and a group of friends convinced the school board to let them do a survey about the planned budget cuts. Based on the survey results, the school board reversed its decision. These two events showed Randi the power of organized labor, the impact of protesting, and how taking a stand can lead to change.

Inspired to make an even greater impact, Randi studied labor relations at Cornell and then went to law school at Yeshiva University. After law school, she got a job at a law firm. But soon she left the corporate world to work for the United Federation of Teachers. "I was a very successful associate at my law firm," says Randi. But her work didn't feel like it had much meaning. It was just one big company fighting another big company. "To have an opportunity to work in education, it just wasn't a difficult choice," says Randi.

As a union organizer, Randi fights for causes like school safety, teacher training, and fair teacher salaries. Randi believes in listening closely to teachers so she can support them in their goals. To better understand the everyday responsibilities and stresses of being a teacher, Randi got a job teaching at a Brooklyn high school. That experience helped her become a better advocate. Over time, Randi took on higher-profile roles in the teacher unions until she became president of the American Federation of Teachers, with 1.7 million members.

Judaism long inspired Randi's commitment to labor organizing. That commitment only grew deeper when she married Rabbi Sharon Kleinbaum. Randi says, "From my earliest days at Camp Ramah to my marriage to a rabbi, I have developed a deep Jewish belief in social justice that has led me to a life of trade unionism."

Randi Weingarten campaigned for . . .

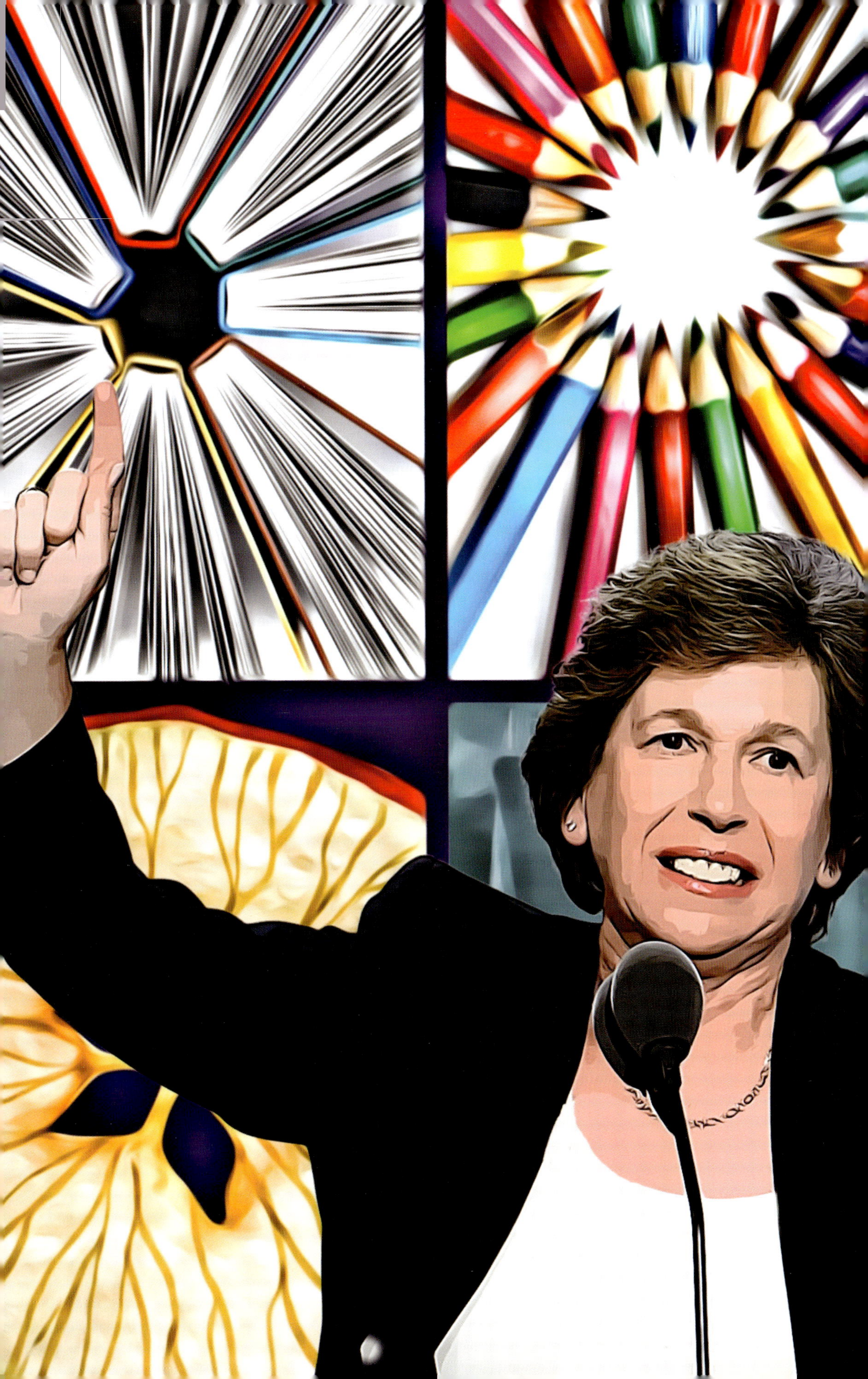

Bernie Sanders

Senator Committed to Economic Equity, 1941-

Bernie first ran for president at age 17—student body president of George Mason High School in Brooklyn. His opponents made campaign promises like better school lunches and cheaper school basketball tickets. Bernie ran on a platform of raising scholarship money for Korean war orphans. Bernie lost the election, but his classmates still helped him raise money for the orphans. Bernie learned an important lesson: even a failed campaign can raise awareness of important issues.

As a boy, Bernie quickly noticed that a lot of things in the world weren't fair. He watched his parents work hard and just barely get by. Growing up in the shadow of World War II, Bernie heard about relatives murdered by the Nazis. "A guy named Adolf Hitler won an election in 1932 . . . 50 million people died as a result of that election in World War II, including six million Jews. So what I learned as a little kid is that politics is, in fact, very important," says Bernie.

Bernie studied political science at the University of Chicago but spent more time on activism than studying. The university still segregated its dorms by race. Bernie organized a sit-in to protest that policy. For several weeks, Bernie and 32 other students camped outside the university president's office. That summer, the University of Chicago integrated its dorms. The victory inspired Bernie toward more activism.

After college, Bernie volunteered on Kibbutz Shaar Ha'amakim near Haifa, Israel. The kibbutzniks shared all work and wealth, an approach to living called socialism. Bernie thought it made a lot of sense. Later, he called himself a democratic socialist when running for office. Back in the United States, Bernie moved to Vermont and, in 1981, ran for mayor of Burlington. He won by 10 votes. Serving as mayor for four terms, he built affordable housing, parks, bike paths, and a vibrant arts scene. In 1991, Bernie was elected to Congress. He won reelection seven times. In 2007, he was first elected to the Senate.

Bernie ran for president twice—in 2016 and 2020. Although he lost both times, Bernie came closer to the Oval Office than any other Jewish candidate. His failed presidential bids raised awareness about issues that are important to him. Dedicated to closing the gap between rich and poor, Bernie is an icon for change. Outspoken and genuine, Bernie might just be the nation's favorite Jewish uncle.

Bernie Sanders served for 22 years on Capitol Hill with . . .

Bernie or Bust
FEEL THE BERN
Bernie
FEEL
ברני

Joseph Lieberman

Orthodox Senator & Israel Advocate, 1942-

As a child, Joe lived in a small house that was wedged between a junkyard and railroad tracks in Stamford, Connecticut. His family was Orthodox. His cousins lived across the street and their synagogue was nearby. Joe, his sisters and parents lived with his grandmother to save money. Joe says his grandparents came to America hoping for opportunity. "But even they could not have dreamed that their grandson would end up a U.S. senator and a barrier-breaking candidate for vice president," says Joe. "But that is America."

Joe won his first election in high school, serving as class president. A few years later, he was elected prom king. Joe graduated high school as a valedictorian and went off to Yale. He was the first person in his family to go to college. Yale had a quota limiting the number of Jewish students; Joe was one of only 10 Jewish students in his class. Even so, he maintained his Orthodox Jewish lifestyle. He woke up early to pray and arranged for kosher meals in the cafeteria. His classmates had a running joke: Joe Lieberman would be the first Jewish president of the United States. Their prediction nearly came true.

Joe went on to attend Yale Law School. His ambition was politics. He served three terms as a Connecticut State Senator and six years as the state's Attorney General. In 1988, he was elected to the United States Senate. He served as a senator for nearly a quarter century. Joe ran for vice president in the 2000 election alongside presidential candidate Al Gore. He was the first Jewish candidate on a major party ticket. While Joe and Al Gore won the popular vote, they lost the electoral college vote in a highly contested election.

Joe showed the country and the world that you can be a religiously observant Jew and also work in politics. At political events, if kosher food wasn't available, Joe ate vegetarian meals. He did not campaign on Shabbat. On the rare times when Congress met on Friday night or Saturday, Joe stayed for the vote but walked the 4.5 miles back to his home. Joe says, "I never found that my religious observance was an obstacle to my success in politics, and it did give me a chance to educate a lot of non-Jews, and maybe some Jews, on what it meant to be an observant Jew."

Joseph Lieberman voted in the Senate to confirm Supreme Court Justice . . .

Ruth Bader Ginsburg

Supreme Court Justice & Feminist Leader, 1933–2020

Ruth did everything right. She graduated first in her high school class, first in her class at Cornell University, and first in her class from law school. In high school, she was the treasurer of the "Go-Getters" club. Yes, Ruth was a go-getter. But when she graduated from law school in 1959, she couldn't find a job. Not a single law firm in all of New York would hire her. Why? Because she was a woman.

Ruth had faced discrimination in the past. At Harvard Law School, there were only nine women in a class of 500. Even so, the dean questioned why these few women should take a spot away from a man. Even though she did well in high school, college, and law school, nothing prepared Ruth for rejection after rejection as she looked for a job. What does a go-getter do if she can't get a job? She pledges to change the system.

Eventually, a judge agreed to hire Ruth as a clerk. Later, she found a teaching position at Rutgers Law School. There, Ruth's students asked her to teach a class on gender discrimination. This fueled Ruth's resolve to be a changemaker. Ruth directed the Women's Rights Project at the American Civil Liberties Union. She argued six cases about gender equality in front of the U.S. Supreme Court and won five of them.

In 1993, President Bill Clinton nominated Ruth herself for the Supreme Court. Ruth introduced herself for her Supreme Court confirmation with these words: "I am . . . a Brooklynite, born and bred—a first-generation American on my father's side, barely second-generation on my mother's. Neither of my parents had the means to attend college, but both taught me to love learning, to care about people, and to work hard for whatever I wanted or believed in."

The Senate confirmed her nomination in a vote of 96 to 3. Ruth became the second female justice in Supreme Court history. Ruth served on the Supreme Court for 27 years, where she showed strong support for justice and equality. Because of the discrimination that she had faced in her education and career, Ruth forged her own path—one full of purpose. As Ruth said, "Real change, enduring change, happens one step at a time."

Before becoming a Supreme Court Justice,
Ruth Bader Ginsburg argued a case in front of the
Supreme Court with . . .

צדק צדק תרדף
EQUAL JUSTICE UNDER LAW

Joe Levin, Jr.

Leading Civil Rights Attorney, 1943–

As a young boy in Montgomery, Alabama, Joe was already on his way to becoming a lawyer. If his friends weren't playing fair on the playground, Joe argued with them. He knew the rules and wanted all the kids to follow them.

As he grew up, Joe learned an important but difficult lesson about his hometown. His neighbors didn't like it if you were poor or Black. Some neighbors even thought that poor, Black people were less human than those who were white. But many of Joe's friends were poor people of color. He didn't like seeing them mistreated. Once, as a gift, Joe's grandmother took him to New York to see Mickey Mantle play baseball. Joe saw Black people sitting with white people in a baseball stadium. He had never seen that at home. In Alabama, nearly everything was segregated. Blacks and whites had separate schools. On buses, white people sat in the front. Even public water fountains were labeled "Black" or "White." Joe began to wonder: Why did Blacks and whites need to be kept separate? Joe respected the need for rules. But what if some rules were wrong?

When Joe studied at the University of Alabama, the school only admitted white students. His friend Melvin Meyer was editor of the student newspaper and wrote editorials supporting integration of the school. Other students—and even the school administration—harassed Melvin for his views. Joe saw what Melvin experienced and it inspired him to fight for equal rights.

Joe went to law school and then started an organization called the Southern Poverty Law Center (SPLC) with his friends Morris Dees and Julian Bond. The SPLC's purpose is quite simple: to seek justice for people who are not able to get justice on their own. Joe's Jewish values guided his work: people were created equally, all in the image of God, regardless of the color of their skin or the religion they practiced. As the SPLC's legal director, Joe worked on 50 major civil rights cases. He helped integrate the YMCA in Montgomery and the Alabama State Troopers. He fought for equal pay for women and men in the military. Several of the SPLC's cases went all the way to the Supreme Court. Joe and the SPLC even made the brave decision to sue the Ku Klux Klan.

These days, the SPLC fights hate, seeks justice, and educates people about civil rights. It helps thousands of people each year. And it all started with a boy named Joe who liked to argue.

Joe Levin used the law to advocate for racial equality.
Who used the law to advocate for women's rights?

Simone Veil

Esteemed European Parliament President, 1927–2017

When the Nazis invaded France in 1940, Simone's family changed their last name from Jacob to Jacquier so they wouldn't stick out. Even so, Simone was arrested the day after she took her university entrance exams. Simone and her sister and mother were deported to Auschwitz. "I am still haunted by the images, the odors, the cries, the humiliation, the blows, and the sky filled with the smoke of the crematoriums," said Simone. Her mother, father and brother did not survive the Holocaust. "I'm often asked what gave me the strength and will to continue the fight. I believe deeply that it was my mother; she has never stopped being present to me, next to me."

Although devastated by the loss of her family, Simone returned to France, determined to study law. She attended the University of Paris, then the Institute of Policy Studies. After practicing law for several years, Simone passed the exam to become a magistrate, a judge responsible for pre-trial investigations. As a magistrate, she devoted herself to prison reform, especially for women, and to women's rights involving child custody and adoption.

In 1974, she became France's Minister of Health. She worked tirelessly for reproductive rights, leading the charge in the French Parliament to legalize abortion. Simone faced tremendous criticism from French Parliament members and the public for her views on reproductive rights. She endured antisemitic threats and swastikas painted on her car. But Simone stuck with it. In 1975, the members of parliament passed *Loi Veil* (Veil's Law), legalizing abortion. Today, many French citizens consider *Loi Veil* to be a cornerstone of their democracy.

As a Holocaust survivor, Simone believed that the countries of Europe needed to work more closely together to guarantee lasting peace. In 1979, Simone was elected to the newly formed European Parliament and became its first president. She served in the European Parliament for 14 years, supporting issues ranging from the environment to public health to human rights.

Late in her life, Simone was elected to the Académie Française, a prestigious organization that oversees the French language. Each member receives a ceremonial sword. Simone had three things engraved on her sword: the motto of the French Republic, the motto of the European Union, and the number 78651. That's the number the Nazis tattooed on her arm at Auschwitz.

Simone Veil survived the Holocaust. So did . . .

RUE SIMONE VEIL
1927-2017
Rescapée de la Shoah
Femme d'Etat
résidente du Parlement européen
MERCI SIMONE

Simon Wiesenthal

Holocaust Survivor & Nazi Hunter, 1908-2005

After surviving five concentration camps, Simon had a mission: find Nazi criminals and bring them to justice. Before the Holocaust, Simon was a young, successful architect in Ukraine. He had married his high school sweetheart, Cyla, and life was good. After the Holocaust, Simon weighed 100 pounds and could hardly walk. Although both he and Cyla survived, they lost 98 relatives to the Nazi horror. "When history looks back," said Simon, "I want people to know the Nazis weren't able to kill millions of people and get away with it."

Once he regained enough of his strength, Simon went to work with the United States Army to gather evidence against the Nazis. To expand his efforts, Simon established the Jewish Historical Documentation Center (JHDC) with 30 other volunteers in Linz, Austria. They gathered a vast collection of evidence against the Nazis. But as time passed, the United States Army had new priorities and the volunteers at JHDC moved on to new projects.

In 1954, Simon sent most of the JHDC files to the Yad Vashem Holocaust Memorial in the new state of Israel. But he saved one file for himself: Adolf Eichmann, the Nazi officer in charge of deporting Jews across Europe to Auschwitz and other extermination camps. Simon needed to find Eichmann. Through careful detective work, Simon followed Eichmann's trail through Europe and across the Atlantic Ocean—all the way to Buenos Aires, Argentina. Like many Nazis, Eichmann found refuge in South America. There, Eichmann had taken the name Ricardo Klement and was working at an automobile plant. In 1960, the Israeli secret police arrested Eichmann, partly because of Simon's information. They brought him to Israel for trial. Eichmann was convicted of crimes against humanity. He was executed in 1962.

Simon continued his work. He spent decades carefully reading documents and talking to informers, survivors, and even former Nazis. He saw his work as a way to prevent future atrocities. "For evil to flourish, it only requires good men to do nothing," said Simon. He had an enormous task. German war-crime files contained 90,000 names. Eventually, Simon provided evidence against 1,100 Nazi war criminals, including Karl Silberbauer, who had arrested Anne Frank.

In 2003, at the age of 95, Simon retired. He had hunted Nazis for over 50 years. Upon his retirement, he said, "I found the mass murderers I was looking for, and I have outlived all of them."

Simon Wiesenthal studied architecture, but World War II derailed his career. Who else studied architecture?

Adolf
Eichmann
Franz Stangl,
commandant
Sobibor
Hermine
Karl

Moshe Safdie

Architect who Transformed Jerusalem, 1938–

Growing up in Haifa, Israel, Moshe and his friends had a plan. Israel had just declared its statehood. They would serve together in the Israel Defense Forces and then establish their own kibbutz. Moshe, who already had experience raising bees and chickens at home, would study agriculture and farm the land.

That all changed when Moshe was 15. His parents, immigrants from Lebanon and Syria, faced financial struggles. They moved the family to Montreal, Canada. Studying agriculture no longer made sense. "I was uprooted," he says. "It seemed extremely traumatic to leave Israel in its infancy, being an ardent Zionist and socialist—if a 15-year-old can be that, and I was."

A high school aptitude test showed Moshe had strengths in art and mathematics. An advisor suggested he study architecture, so he did. For his senior thesis at McGill University, Moshe created a model urban development. Influenced by memories of kibbutz communities and Arab villages, Moshe designed a multi-family community where each unit was built on top of another but had garden space and felt like an individual home. Moshe used white Lego bricks to build a model, buying out most of the Lego bricks in Montreal in the process. Moshe presented his design at Montreal's World Exposition of 1967. The organizers chose to build it. This launched Moshe's world-class career as an architect.

Moshe has designed over 75 projects worldwide, including a mosque in Dubai, Singapore's Jewel Changi Airport, and six Canadian museums and libraries. Moshe's designs have dramatic curves, geometric patterns, and carefully placed green spaces. "I think you need to, as an architect, understand the essence of a place and create a building that feels like it resonates with the culture of a place," says Moshe.

He refines his designs while listening to music for inspiration. For example, when designing a Jerusalem yeshiva, Moshe listened to music from Israeli synagogues. While he's a global architect, Moshe works extensively in Israel. Among his Israeli projects, Moshe designed the Holocaust History Museum at Yad Vashem, Ben-Gurion Airport, and the Yitzhak Rabin Center. Moshe spent 40 years on projects linking Jerusalem's new and old cities.

As a child, Moshe dreamt of farming Israel's land. Instead, he built it up. What is the secret of his success? Moshe says, "Who knows, maybe I am simply a talented architect?"

Moshe Safdie never intended to be an architect.
Neither did . . .

Frank Gehry

Visionary International Architect, 1929–

Frank loved working in his grandfather's hardware store as a young boy in Toronto, Canada. The aisles of supplies were a creative playground to him. He brought home an endless supply of wood scraps. Each weekend, Frank and his grandmother built miniature cities on the living room floor out of the scraps. In his imagination, their creations were soaring towers and stunning balconies. Frank's mother took him to museums and concerts, sparking his love of art and music. Frank's grandfather studied Talmud with him, encouraging him to be inquisitive. "It's about curiosity. And I think that is really important. You've got to be curious," says Frank.

When Frank was a teenager, his family fell on hard financial times. His uncle moved them to Los Angeles for a fresh start. There, Frank drove a delivery truck, struggling to find a career path. He says, "Just on a hunch, I tried some architecture classes." Frank majored in architecture at the University of Southern California, then studied at Harvard and did an internship in Paris. Ambitious to make it in the architectural world, Frank changed his last name from Goldberg to Gehry to avoid antisemitism. He later regretted that choice.

As an architect, Frank is known for using inexpensive building supplies in surprising, creative, and artistic ways. He once built an entire furniture line out of cardboard! Frank's first well-known project was his own home in Santa Monica. He wrapped the whole house in metal. Soon so many tour buses drove by his home to see it that he did a second renovation to add more privacy. Frank built an international reputation by designing the Guggenheim Museum in Bilboa, Spain. After that, several cities commissioned Frank to design buildings, like the Walt Disney Concert Hall in Los Angeles. At one point, Frank had a staff of 160 people working for him, but he still oversaw the design of each building himself.

Frank has always felt more comfortable with artists than architects. "I approach each building as a sculptural object, a spatial container, a space with light and air," says Frank. When he won the prestigious Pritzker Prize, the committee compared him to Picasso.

And it all started with a boy named Frank building imaginary cities in the living room with his beloved grandmother.

Frank Gehry is inspired by nature.
So is . . .

Amit Goffer

INVENTOR OF STANDING WHEELCHAIR, 1953–

Life was good for Amit. He married, had three children and founded a technology company. "I admit that I hadn't give much thought to people who are paralyzed or in a wheelchair," says Amit. But that changed one tragic day in 1997. For a bit of fun with his children, Amit rented all-terrain vehicles (ATVs). Amit and his daughter shared one ATV and took off into the wilderness near their home in the north of Israel. Suddenly their ATV's brakes failed. Amit and his daughter were thrown off. Thankfully, his daughter was not injured, but Amit's spinal cord injuries left him a quadriplegic. He could no longer use his arms and legs.

After months of rehabilitation, Amit went home, confined to a wheelchair. His body was paralyzed, but his mind was not. He began researching different types of wheelchairs and was stunned at the lack of innovation. "I couldn't understand why the wheelchair was the only solution for the paralyzed," says Amit.

Scouring the internet for answers, Amit read an article about scorpions and their exoskeleton—a support system outside their bodies. While many people are afraid of scorpions, Amit was fascinated by them. While studying scorpions, it was as if a light bulb turned on in Amit's head. "How is it possible that no one ever thought of this?" he wondered. Amit became obsessed with designing a mechanical exoskeleton for people confined to wheelchairs. It took seven years, but Amit designed ReWalk—a motorized robotic support suit that allows paraplegics to walk.

Unfortunately, because Amit can't use his arms, he was unable to use his own invention. Amit continued to research and innovate. Amit designed UPnRIDE, a wheelchair that allows quadriplegics like him to stand. "The dignity, self-esteem. To feel like part of society again, the core of society, not the fringe of society—the psychological effect is dramatic," says Amit.

Amit's inventions have not been commercial successes—at least not yet. But for the hundreds of people who do use them, Amit's inventions have been life-changing. He has successfully engineered independence and improved personal dignity. As for Amit? Using UPnRIDE, he was able to stand under the *chuppah* at two of his children's weddings.

Amit Goffer did not let personal hardships stop him.
Neither did . . .

Barbara Walters

Celebrated Broadcast Journalist, 1929-2022

"Can you tell me about your childhood?"

Barbara, a legendary broadcast journalist, began hundreds of interviews with this question. It was one of her favorite ways to start an interview, and Barbara interviewed everybody from presidents to convicted criminals to rock stars. Barbara said that beginning with this question put the other person at ease. But more importantly, it allowed for a fascinating follow-up question: "How does your childhood impact you today?"

Barbara herself had neither the most normal nor the happiest childhood. Her father owned a chain of night clubs called the Latin Quarter. The family moved a lot, and this was lonely. But Barbara also met a lot of celebrities. She grew up among showgirls, musicians, and comedians. She didn't see any glamour in being famous. She learned that "behind these fantasy figures were real people." When she started interviewing celebrities, Barbara didn't feel shy or intimidated like some people might.

Because her family moved so often, Barbara was especially close to her older sister, Jacqueline. "She was the most significant part of my life," said Barbara. Jacqueline had developmental disabilities and Barbara watched her struggle. "If I think about the positive from the experience, it gave me compassion and an understanding of people that I might never have had," she said. She traced her success as a journalist back to this sensitivity.

Barbara's first professional break came in 1961, writing for *The Today Show*. Barbara wanted to cover hard news, but the producers offered her an opportunity to appear on air as a "Today Girl." She just needed to look attractive, make small talk, and read commercials. Finally, she convinced NBC to allow her to travel with First Lady Jacqueline Kennedy to India and Pakistan to report on the trip. By 1964, Barbara regularly appeared on *The Today Show*. It took another decade for Barbara to officially be called a co-host of the show. By then, the network had no other option; viewers were demanding Barbara get more on-air time. As her career progressed, she hosted the news program *20/20* and launched *The View*, a talk show with a panel of female hosts.

After more than 50 years on air, Barbara Walters announced her retirement in 2014. She said, "I do not want to appear on another program or climb another mountain. I want instead to sit on a sunny field and admire the very gifted women—and OK, some men, too—who will be taking my place."

Barbara Walters interviewed . . .

Gloria Steinem

Journalist & Feminist Activist, 1934–

Gloria was born in Ohio. Her family traveled the country with her father, who sold antiques from a trailer. The family moved so often that Gloria didn't finish a complete school year at one school until she was 12 years old. When Gloria's mother began suffering from mental illness, her father could not handle it. Her parents divorced and her father left. Gloria cared for her ailing mother on her own, even tap dancing at a local club for $10 a night to support them. Thankfully, Gloria's older sister stepped in and brought Gloria to live with her in Washington, DC.

Away from her difficult family circumstances, Gloria excelled at school and dreamed about the future. She attended Smith College and studied in Switzerland and England, graduating with top honors. After college, she spent two years in India on a fellowship, learning about community organizing and immersing herself in the nonviolent philosophy of Mahatma Gandhi. Gloria decided she wanted to be a journalist. She returned to the United States and settled in New York City, ready to write important articles about social change. Gloria quickly learned that most publications hired women to write only about fashion and gossip. So Gloria looked for creative ways to write important stories, even going undercover to investigate sexism in the workplace.

After years of fighting to write what she wanted, Gloria had her opportunity. She became a founding editor of *Ms. Magazine*, the first mass market feminist publication. She also became a prominent spokesperson for the feminist movement in the 1960s and 1970s, advocating for the Equal Rights Amendment, co-founding the Women's Action Alliance and, later, helping to establish Take Our Daughters to Work Day. She wrote and lectured about racism, sexism, violence toward women, and how strict gender roles stunt children's development.

Although she was never observant, Gloria has a strong, proud Jewish identity. While Gloria's father was Jewish, it was her mother, who wasn't Jewish, who emphasized having Jewish pride. "Never in my life have I identified myself as a Christian, but wherever there is antisemitism, I identify as a Jew," says Gloria.

These days, while in her 80s, Gloria continues to write and fight for social change. She can't imagine not working. What's her advice to young people today? Dream big. In her words: "Dreaming, after all, is a form of planning."

Gloria Steinem is a master community organizer.
So is . . .

Stosh Cotler

Activist & Community Mobilizer, 1968–

When Stosh was growing up in Olympia, Washington, she didn't think she had a place in Judaism. She went to a school with very few Jews and, most days, she just wanted to fit in. She says, "My family was on the fast track to assimilation, and by high school, being Jewish was simply a reminder that I was an outsider."

After high school, Stosh moved to Portland, Oregon. Her friends were activists, musicians, and artists. Many, like Stosh, were members of the LGBTQ community. Stosh developed a reputation as a radical social activist. A black belt in Kung Fu, she founded an organization to teach self-defense and anti-violence to women and girls. Seeking spirituality, she explored Buddhism but felt distant from Judaism. Then one Passover, acquaintances invited Stosh to their Seder. Stosh hesitated to attend but felt more comfortable when she arrived and saw a rainbow pride flag next to the mezuzah.

"We began the evening reading from the hand-made Haggadah prepared for the Seder, written specifically because so many of these people had been invisibilized, marginalized, traumatized or otherwise neglected by their mainstream Jewish upbringing," says Stosh. "I truly felt like I had found my 'home' in those short hours at the Seder. . . . That Seder marked my return to Judaism and the beginning of my conscious and proud identity as a Jew."

Stosh began studying and going to synagogue. At age 30, Stosh celebrated a bat mitzvah. She merged her dedication to social justice with her Jewish identity, speaking out for peace in Israel and advocating for Palestinian rights. She moved to New York to work for the Jewish Fund for Justice, which later became Bend the Arc. Over the years, she took on more responsibility until she became CEO. With Stosh as a leader, Bend the Arc tripled its staff and opened offices in six more cities. "My purpose in life, if I look back at where I come from, has consistently been to create more space for more people to live free and safe and with dignity," says Stosh.

Stosh found her way in Judaism through activism. She fights hard for those who can't fight for themselves while mobilizing others to join the fight, too.

Stosh Cotler grew up in Washington state. So did . . .

Angela Warnick Buchdahl

Korean-American Rabbi, 1972–

Angela's mother hurried around the kitchen, preparing for the Passover Seder. She put the ritual items on the Seder plate: roasted egg, parsley, shankbone . . . *kimchee?* Angela's mother, a Korean Buddhist, saw the spicy kimchee as an excellent alternative to horseradish for the maror, the bitter herbs. Their family merged their Jewish and Korean identities; why shouldn't their Seder plate? Angela, whose father is an American Jew, says, "I think many people think, wow, you represent the new face of Judaism in some way. And I would say, actually, if you look back across Jewish history, we've always been a diverse people."

Angela's parents met when her father was stationed at a military base in Seoul, South Korea. Her mother's Korean lineage goes all the back to King Taejo in the 9th century, whose dynasty lasted 500 years. When Angela was five, her family moved from Korea to Tacoma, Washington, where her father's ancestors helped found the synagogue a century earlier. As a child, Angela asked many questions about God—something she continues to do today. "I got the best of my mother's spiritual questioning, curiosity, and worldview, combined with my father's Jewish vocabulary," says Angela.

Angela's congregation in Tacoma fully embraced Angela and her family. Elsewhere, though, she experienced prejudice that made her wonder whether she belonged in the Jewish community. At age 16, Angela traveled to Israel to study. There, other students questioned whether she was really Jewish because of her mother's background. "The rejection was so painful that I couldn't tell the story for a really long time without crying," recalls Angela.

After talking with her mother, Angela said she came to realize "I could no sooner stop being a Jew than I could stop being Korean, or female, or me." She chose to reaffirm her Jewish identity through a formal conversion when she was 21. She saw it more as a ceremony of reaffirmation.

After college at Yale, Angela went to cantorial and rabbinical school. She is the first Asian-American rabbi or cantor, but she's quick to say she won't be the last. Today, she is senior rabbi at New York City's Central Synagogue, one of the country's most influential synagogues. Her passionate interpretations of Jewish music bring people from all over the world to her services, which are also broadcast all over the world. Even in Seoul.

Angela Warnick Buchdahl delights in merging her different identities. So does . . .

Michael Twitty

AWARD-WINNING FOOD HISTORIAN, 1977–

As a boy, Michael looked forward to Fridays. Although Christian, his mom would buy fresh-baked challah, toast it, and serve it with blackberry jam and apple butter—condiments of her Southern heritage. The challah was delicious and filled Michael with a sweet feeling about Judaism.

Michael's grandmother also had a connection to Jewish food. She worked as a cook for a Jewish family and brought Jewish recipes home. With his mother's toasted challah and his grandmother's recipes, food introduced Michael to Judaism.

When he was seven, Michael watched *The Chosen*, a coming-of-age movie about a Jewish boy. "I was fascinated by the movie and thought, wow, I can relate to this spiritual thing," said Michael. He declared himself Jewish. For a week, he wore a baseball cap as a kippah and didn't eat bacon. Then his mother told him there was more to being Jewish than that. Michael was curious about Judaism, but it was many years before he officially converted.

As a young adult, Michael was fascinated by food history. While interning at the Smithsonian Institution, Michael met Jewish cookbook author Joan Nathan. She sent him to find a recipe at a nearby Sephardic congregation. When he arrived, an African American man greeted him. Michael took it as a sign. Michael started attending services there. He converted to Judaism when he was 25. "That was one of the few places I could go where I felt like my complete self was being nourished," said Michael.

Michael identifies as Jewish, Black, and gay. He says, "This makes my soul's recipe unique and powerful." He traces his ancestry to African slaves from Ghana and Sierra Leone and white slave owners. Researching the history of food is a gateway into his slave ancestors' culture. "They took our names, they took our gods, they took our religion—but they didn't take our food," he said.

Today, Michael is a well-known food historian. Michael's first book, *The Cooking Gene*, won two James Beard Awards, the most prestigious prize for food writing. Michael sees food history as a vehicle for social change. Once, Michael told an Israeli and Palestinian audience that neither group can claim ownership of hummus. Rather, a common ancestor holds that distinction. Michael said, "Hummus belongs to a Mesopotamian woman—neither Jewish nor Muslim—who had hungry kids. And she had some chickpeas and some garlic—she mashed them together and said, 'Here, eat!'"

Michael Twitty chose Judaism as an adult. So did . . .

Rachel Cowan

Trailblazing Rabbi for Inclusion, 1941–2018

In 1963, Rachel had just finished social work school and was eager to make a difference in the world. She went to rural Maryland where the public schools had recently been integrated. There, she devoted herself to tutoring African American students to prepare them for their new schools. As Rachel tutored her students, she noticed a young journalist named Paul interviewing people. He had come from New York to report on integration efforts. Rachel and Paul became friends. Over time, they fell in love and got married.

Although they shared many values, Rachel and Paul had different backgrounds. Paul's family was Jewish. Rachel's family was Protestant and traced its ancestry directly back to the Pilgrims on the *Mayflower*. "As a teenager in Wellesley, Massachusetts, I was inspired by my Quaker summer camp and my Unitarian Church youth movement, as well as my parents' New England Protestant values, to become a social justice activist, civil rights worker, Peace Corps volunteer, feminist, birdwatcher. A good person," said Rachel.

Back then, interfaith marriage was far less common than it is today. But Rachel and Paul knew they could make their marriage work. Inspired by their shared commitment to social justice, they went to Mississippi to register African American voters and to Ecuador with the Peace Corps to help people in that country. When they had children, they moved to the Upper West Side of New York City. Rachel, Paul, and their children went to synagogue and embraced Judaism.

Trailblazers, Rachel and Paul wanted to make the Jewish community more open, accepting, and supportive to interfaith couples. They wrote a groundbreaking book called *Mixed Blessings* to help guide other families like them. Eventually, Rachel chose to convert and to study to be a rabbi. Tragically, before Rachel was ordained, Paul died of leukemia. In mourning, Rachel focused her energies on spirituality. Drawing on Jewish texts, mental health practices, and other faith traditions, Rachel pioneered the Jewish healing movement, creating healing services and circles.

After a lifetime of making a difference in the world, Rachel offered this advice to others: "You don't have to be Ben-Gurion or Golda Meir or Gandhi or Martin Luther King. You just have to be your most authentic, courageous, and inspiring self and to trust your heart."

Rachel Cowan was a Freedom Rider. So was . . .

Andrew Goodman

Freedom Rider & Martyr for Civil Rights, 1943–1964

Sitting as a passenger in the car, Andrew could see the sheriff signaling the driver to pull over. A college student from New York City, Andrew had arrived that day in Mississippi to help register Black citizens to vote. He had been warned that the police harassed Freedom Summer volunteers. The other two civil rights workers in the car, James Chaney, a Black Mississippian, and Michael Schwerner, a fellow Jewish activist from New York, were far more experienced. Andrew had joined them to investigate the burning of an African American church, a site for voter registration. It was one of 20 churches that the Ku Klux Klan burned that summer.

James had no choice but to pull over. The sheriff—who was a member of the KKK—accused James of speeding and arrested all three men. Andrew, James, and Michael spent six hours in Meridian, Mississippi's jail. At 10 o'clock that evening, the jailer let them go and told them to leave the county. As they drove out of town, the KKK was waiting for them. The three men were not seen alive again. Two days later, their burned-out station wagon was discovered. Almost two months later, the FBI found their buried bodies.

Andrew's decision to participate in Freedom Summer had not been a surprise. He grew up in a family devoted to social activism. While Andrew originally planned to major in drama in college and had even acted in Off-Broadway productions, he had become more interested in politics and had recently switched his major to anthropology. When John Lewis, who later became a prominent congressman, recruited Andrew for Freedom Summer, Andrew eagerly volunteered. Andrew felt white northerners could be "shockingly apathetic" and wanted to do something that mattered.

Andrew lived a short life. But the good work he started continues. In 1966, Andrew's parents, Robert and Carolyn Goodman, started The Andrew Goodman Foundation. In 2014, on the 50th anniversary of the murders, the Foundation officially launched Vote Everywhere, a program designed to support college students who are continuing the work of Freedom Summer.

Honoring Andrew, James, and Michael, President Barack Obama said, "I am one of the many who stand on the shoulders of giants like Andy. His death forever changed our nation, and in his example, we are reminded of the difference we each can make when we summon up the courage to lift up the lives of others."

Andrew Goodman stood up for his values despite the danger to himself. So did . . .

Harvey Milk

Pioneering Gay Elected Official, 1933–1978

Growing up on Long Island, Harvey's parents taught him to stand up for the underdog. They instilled within him a pride about being Jewish. At Hebrew school, he learned Jewish values like *tikkun olam*, healing the world. Yet Harvey had a secret. By high school, Harvey knew he was gay. And he didn't think that his parents or the Jewish community would accept that.

In college, Harvey joined a Jewish fraternity. He still hid that he was gay. After graduating, Harvey signed up with the Navy and served as a diving instructor in San Diego. His Navy career was successful until the Navy asked him whether he was gay. Gay men and women couldn't serve in the military back then. Harvey resigned.

Harvey moved back to New York. He wasn't sure what he wanted to do next, so he tried different jobs. Harvey worked as a teacher, as a stock analyst, and as an actor on Broadway. His friends knew he was gay, but he hid that part of his identity from his family. He didn't go to synagogue, afraid he wouldn't be accepted. But he liked speaking Yiddish and cracking Jewish jokes. He cooked Jewish foods for his friends and each year, he attended a Passover Seder.

In 1972, Harvey moved to San Francisco and opened a camera shop on Castro Street, the heart of the city's active gay community. He hung his bar mitzvah picture on the store's wall. Harvey became an outspoken leader for the gay community and helped organize lesbian and gay business owners. Harvey became known as "Mayor of Castro Street."

Harvey ran for the San Francisco Board of Supervisors and lost. He kept trying. The third time, Harvey won. He became one of the nation's first openly gay elected officials. Harvey saw his role as larger than gay and lesbian issues. He sponsored bills to help working mothers, house the poor, and keep the police accountable for their actions.

In 1977, a gay and lesbian synagogue, Sha'ar Zahav, opened in San Francisco. Harvey attended High Holiday services for the first time since childhood. Listening to the familiar melodies felt like coming home.

But Harvey's story ends abruptly and tragically. On November 27, 1978, a former city supervisor, who had clashed with Harvey, snuck into City Hall with a gun. He shot and killed Harvey and Mayor George Moscone. Harvey's death galvanized the gay rights movement. "Harvey Milk lives!" became a rallying call across the nation.

Harvey Milk worked toward gay acceptance.
So does . . .

MILK
HARVEY
MILK
HARVEY

Eytan Fox

INNOVATIVE ISRAELI FILM DIRECTOR, 1964–

As a boy in Jerusalem, Eytan Fox knew far too well the stereotype of the strong and tough Israeli man. "I grew up with that man, with that myth. He's on my shoulder, on my back, he's connected to me from all directions," says Eytan.

Eytan, like his friends, tried to be that man. He served in the Israel Defense Forces, of course; most young adults in Israel do. He was physically fit and confident. But still he wondered whether he could be that ideal Israeli man. Eytan is artistic. And gay. So what does an artistic, gay Israeli do when he finishes his army duty? He studies to become a filmmaker and makes movies about being Israeli, gay, and conflicted.

To date, Eytan has directed eight movies and several television shows. He has won 28 international film awards and his films have been released in over 30 countries. All of Eytan's films reflect something about his life. For one of his first projects in film school, Eytan told the story of his parents' divorce when he was 10. Making that short movie showed Eytan the emotional power of being a filmmaker.

Nearly all his films include homosexual characters. Through his films, Eytan has helped crack the stereotype of the rough and tough Israeli male, revealing a more diverse and realistic image. Eytan himself knows the uncertainty of revealing your true self. "While at Tel Aviv University I had a partner, and I felt strong enough to say to friends and family: 'This is the life I've chosen and I want you to love me for it,'" says Eytan. When Eytan told his father he was gay, it wasn't easy for his father to accept at first, but eventually he did.

Eytan also explores Jewish and Palestinian relations in his films. He tends to focus on friendships and romantic relationships between Jewish and Arab characters rather than larger political issues. In an often-segregated country, Eytan grew up with both Jewish and Arab friends. Eytan's mother served on the Jerusalem City Council and worked closely with Palestinians from East Jerusalem. She often invited her Palestinian friends to Shabbat dinner and they became Eytan's friends, too.

After Eytan had made several movies in Israel, he went to Hollywood, thinking it would be good for his career. He soon realized his life's mission was in Israel: he was meant to make Israeli films about Israeli society. Eytan left Hollywood behind and came home.

Eytan Fox incorporates Krav Maga into his movies, a martial arts system created by . . .

Emerich "Imi" Lichtenfeld

Martial Artist, Founder of Krav Maga, 1910–1998

Imi was a powerful athlete. Growing up in Bratislava, Slovakia, he excelled at sports, from swimming to ballroom dancing. Strong, muscular, and swift, he won national and international medals in wrestling, boxing, and gymnastics. Imi's role model was his father—a former circus acrobat, chief inspector of the Bratislava police force, and owner of the Hercules Gymnasium, where Imi trained.

In the mid-1930s, Bratislava began to change.

Fascist and antisemitic gangs regularly attacked Jews on the streets. Imi was forced to use his athletic skills for another purpose: self-defense. He was in countless street fights, his reputation rising to celebrity status in the Jewish quarter. "I began fighting antisemitism in the 30s. When the Hitler youth gangs used to single out Jewish young men on the streets, it was either hit or run. I found the hitting more satisfying," said Imi.

Imi quickly realized that the required skills for sports competitions were different than those for real-life self-defense. He brought together Jewish boxers and wrestlers. Together, the group developed a system for practical self-defense, combining skills from various sports and emphasizing natural movement and self-restraint. Eventually, Imi's system of self-defense evolved into a new martial arts form called Krav Maga (which literally means "contact combat" in Hebrew).

By 1940, Imi was so famous as a fighter in Bratislava that his safety was in jeopardy. Imi fled on the last immigrant ship to escape the Nazis for British Mandate Palestine. The ship, the Pencho, was overcrowded and in terrible condition. It shipwrecked in the Greek islands. Imi didn't make it to Palestine for two years. When Imi finally got there, military leaders immediately recognized his fighting prowess and recruited him to train Jewish fighters.

When the state of Israel was declared in 1948, Imi became chief instructor for physical fitness in the Israel Defense Forces (IDF). He served in the IDF for 20 years, refining the techniques of Krav Maga for soldiers, the police, and regular citizens of all ages and abilities.

"What I was teaching was a unique combination of judo, karate, aikido, kung fu and boxing," said Imi.

Imi lost nearly his whole family in the Holocaust. He dedicated his life to teaching self-defense. When asked why he developed Krav Maga, Imi simply answered, "So one may walk in peace."

Imi Lichtenfeld came to British Mandate Palestine to escape the Holocaust. So did . . .

Uzia Galil

Founding Father of High-Tech in Israel, 1925–2021

When Uzia was 16, the Nazis invaded his native country of Romania and young Jews were no longer allowed to attend school. Leaving his parents behind, Uzia joined the last group of Jewish youth allowed to leave Bucharest. He wouldn't see his parents again for a decade. The young refugees took a boat to Turkey, a train through Syria to Lebanon, and finally a bus to British Mandate Palestine. Uzia went to a technical high school. When he graduated, he enrolled in the engineering program at the Technion, Haifa's elite scientific university.

Just before Israel's War of Independence, Uzia graduated from the Technion and joined the Israel Defense Forces. With his engineering knowledge, Uzia was put in charge of radio technology in his unit. After the war, Israel sent its most promising young citizens overseas to pursue more education. Uzia was sent to Purdue University in Indiana for graduate school. When Uzia returned to Israel, he became a chief engineer for the military and a professor at the Technion.

Uzia saw himself as a pioneer, working for Israel and its future. While the country focused on agriculture as its lead industry, Uzia believed Israel's future was technology. And while Israel's military and universities had cutting-edge technology, Israeli companies lagged far behind. Uzia believed that industrial, military, and academic leaders needed to work together.

Uzia launched Elron Electronic Industries as a tiny start-up lab in his home. It became Israel's first multinational technology company with specialties ranging from healthcare to cellular communications to defense. Wanting a thriving technological community, Uzia helped launch the Matam technological park in Haifa. Today, Matam is the Israeli home to Intel, Microsoft, Apple, Google, and more. Finally, he founded Uzia Initiatives and Management to support young Israeli entrepreneurs.

Israel is now one of the most technologically advanced countries in the world. It is often called the "start-up nation." Once a refugee child, Uzia is considered Israel's high-tech founding father. He won the coveted Israel Prize for his huge contribution to Israel's technology development. His colleagues praised him for his modesty, humanity, and vision.

Asked to sum up his life philosophy, Uzia answered quite simply: "Yesterday has already gone. Tomorrow is the future, and I'm always looking ahead."

Uzia Galil was a pioneer in Israel's high-tech "Silicon Wadi."
A key innovator in California's Silicon Valley is . . .

Google

Sheryl Sandberg

TECHNOLOGY EXECUTIVE & AUTHOR , 1969-

By all accounts, Sheryl was born a leader. "To the best of our knowledge Sheryl never actually played as a child but really just organized other children's play," said Sheryl's younger brother and sister at her wedding. Her brother and sister would know. As children, Sheryl taught them to listen to her speak and then "scream the word 'right,'" when she finished.

In high school in Miami Beach, Florida, Sheryl had a tight-knit group of eight friends who were "smart girls" like her—girls who took honors classes and served in student government. Sheryl says that even if they were not invited to the "cool" parties, she and her friends had each other. Decades have passed and Sheryl remains very close to her high school friends. Her friends use words like *commanding*, *personable*, *motivated*, *smart*, and *dynamic* to describe her.

Sheryl's family was active at their synagogue, especially in efforts to free Soviet Jews. Sheryl participated in protest marches, handed out petitions, and worked on letter-writing campaigns. Working on the Soviet Jewry campaign proved to Sheryl that she could make a difference in the world. "My parents taught my siblings and me to be proud of our Jewish heritage and that leading a meaningful life meant doing what you can to make the world a better place," says Sheryl.

Sheryl studied economics at Harvard, then worked at the World Bank and Treasury Department before moving to Silicon Valley to work at Google. In California, Sheryl met Facebook founder Mark Zuckerberg at a party. Sheryl wasn't looking for a job and Mark wasn't looking for a Chief Operating Officer. But Mark thought Sheryl would help make Facebook profitable. Mark's hunch about Sheryl was certainly correct.

As "Second-in-Charge" at Facebook, Sheryl broke glass ceilings in the high-tech world. Dedicated to helping women build their leadership skills, Sheryl wrote *Lean In: Women, Work, and the Will to Lead*. She launched the "lean-in" movement to spread her philosophy: "Women hold ourselves back in ways both big and small, by lacking self-confidence, by not raising our hands, and by pulling back when we should be leaning in."

Time magazine named Sheryl one of the 100 most influential people in the world. Using that influence to support girls and women, she says, "A truly equal world would be one where women ran half our countries and companies, and men ran half our homes."

Sheryl Sandberg has been an important voice in the #MeToo movement. So has . . .

Aly Raisman

Olympic Gymnastic Champion, 1994–

Head held high, Aly walked onto the arena floor at the 2012 London Olympics. While her pose exuded confidence, Aly worked hard inwardly to control her nerves. She stood at the corner of the mat and breathed deeply. Aly knew not to let her anxiety derail her ambition. Still, nothing compared to the stakes of an Olympic competition. Aly had trained for this moment since her first gymnastics class at age three. She had missed family vacations, birthday parties, and even her senior year of high school for a chance at Olympic gold. All the sacrifices led to this moment. Her moment.

Striking her opening pose, lifting her chin to the ceiling, and smiling ever so slightly, Aly waited for the music to begin. Hava Nagila, a Jewish folksong of joy, blared into the arena. In her moment of glory, Aly would not be quiet about her Jewish pride. To the beat of her ancestry and her own heart, Aly took off down the mat, propelling herself into midair twists and flips. By the end of the second tumbling run of the routine, Aly knew it: this was a gold medal-winning performance. She would be an Olympic champion.

When Aly stepped onto the victor's podium that night, she was already a three-time world champion. But this night, Aly's gold medal for her routine was special. Rarely had a Jewish athlete so proudly displayed her heritage. She had become a symbol of Jewish strength.

After the Olympics, Aly would need a different type of strength. She was holding onto a heart-wrenching secret: her gymnastics team doctor had touched her inappropriately on numerous occasions. Many other gymnasts had been hurt by the doctor, too. Aly decided to share her secret and stand up in court. Not letting anxiety stop her, she would tell her story and become an advocate for sexual assault victims. Based on Aly's testimony, as well as those of many other women, the doctor was convicted for abusing at least 265 athletes. Today, Aly encourages other young people not to remain silent about abuse: "Your story matters, you matter, and you should trust yourself."

Aly Raisman has appeared on Dancing with the Stars. So has . . .

Paula Abdul

Energetic Singer, Songwriter & Dancer, 1962–

As a child in Southern California, Paula loved to dance. She would watch Gene Kelly's famous dance routine in *Singing in the Rain* and run up to kiss the television screen. Her dance lessons began soon afterwards. Tap, jazz, ballet, even break dancing—Paula loved them all. "Dance is my truest love and my burning passion," she says. "What a gift to be able to evoke and express joy, curiosity, sensuality, anger."

At the end of Paula's freshman year at college, she was chosen from among 700 young women to be a Los Angeles Lakers cheerleader. Very quickly, Paula became head choreographer for the squad. From there, she began choreographing for the musician Janet Jackson and other stars, including actor Tom Hanks. Eventually, Paula began producing her own music. Paula had six number-one singles in the late 1980s and early 1990s and won multiple Grammys, MTV video music awards, and Emmys. Then, for eight seasons, Paula was a judge on *American Idol*.

As Paula's fame grew, so did her feelings of insecurity. "The confidence I had when I was just plain anonymous Paula eroded," she says. "Suddenly being Paula Abdul was not a very comfortable place to be." For many years, Paula struggled with the eating disorder bulimia. Eventually, Paula sought help and, with therapy, learned to maintain a healthy lifestyle. "There are three things I commit to on a daily basis," she says. "Exercising for an hour a day, tops. Never skipping meals. And accepting the size and shape I was born with."

Paula also relies on Judaism for support. She says, "I treasure the traditions of Judaism. They have grounded me during my most challenging hours when only my faith could hold me to my life's course." Paula's father was a Syrian Jew who grew up in Brazil while her mother was Canadian with Jewish roots. At age 51, Paula fulfilled a lifelong dream of visiting Israel. Since she did not have a bat mitzvah at 13, Paula celebrated her bat mitzvah there. She says, "It was one of my proudest moments. It was a love affair for me. I cried and did not want to leave."

Paula danced and sang her way to stardom. But she found her way to happiness through self-acceptance and faith. Her advice: "Break the rules, stand apart, ignore your head, and follow your heart."

Paula Abdul won two Grammy awards.
Another Grammy-winning musician is . . .

Daveed Diggs

Actor & Rapper, Best Known for Hamilton, 1982-

Riding his bicycle through Los Angeles, Daveed had a lot on his mind and most of it was good. He had tickets to fly east in two days to join the cast of *Hamilton*. Lost in thought, Daveed suddenly saw a police officer. The officer grabbed David off his bicycle and threw him against a fence. Daveed kept his wits about him. His Jewish mom and African American dad had taught him well. When it comes to the police: be polite and keep your hands visible. Daveed walked away traumatized but safe.

Daveed was not surprised by what happened. The police had stopped him for no reason dozens of times before—the price of being a young Black man. Growing up, Daveed envied his white friends. They could goof off and the police would ignore them. Rapping became Daveed's anecdote to racism. Rapping amplified his voice. He says, "I was a poor black kid from east Oakland; nobody had any reason to listen to me. . . . But all of a sudden with this trick of making it sound pretty, everybody was not only hearing you but excited to hear what you were going to say next. That's a very powerful thing for a kid to learn."

After graduating from Brown University, Daveed lived the life of a struggling artist. He pursued only creative projects that interested him, even if it meant bouncing between friends' couches because he couldn't afford an apartment. Then came *Hamilton*. Daveed played Thomas Jefferson and Marquis de Lafayette. He won a Tony and a Grammy. Suddenly, Daveed had fame, money, and invitations to do other creative projects. But it didn't mean that Daveed had to accept everything. When Disney approached Daveed to create a song and video for Hanukkah, his immediate reaction was absolutely not. But then Daveed got talking with Disney and realized they wanted a video featuring Jewish diversity. Daveed agreed to the project. The result was *Puppy for Hanukkah*, a klezmer-rap mashup, featuring Jewish kids of color simply having fun.

When Daveed thinks back on his childhood, what does he remember first? Racism, police profiling, poverty? No. Daveed says, "What I remember is laughing so much my face hurt, and never ever being bored."

Daveed Diggs experienced police harassment.
So did . . .

BROADWAY
Oakland

Jacobo Timerman

Argentine Journalist & Political Dissident , 1923–1999

Jacobo insisted on publishing the names of the *desaparecidos*—the disappeared ones. Despite threatening phone calls and government harassment, he would not back down. In 1976, the military overthrew Argentina's government. In the following years, thousands of activists and students were arrested, including many Jews. Often *desaparecidos* were never heard from again. If Jacobo didn't print their names in his newspaper, *La Opinión*, who would?

Jacobo knew all about being the underdog. Born in Ukraine, Jacobo left with his parents when he was just five. Antisemitic riots called pogroms had made Ukraine unsafe. His family settled half a world away in Buenos Aires. Life wasn't easy. When Jacobo was 12, his father died. Jacobo, his mother, and brother moved into a one-room apartment. In exchange for rent, they worked as the building's janitors.

Jacobo saw his family's struggles as the struggle of working people everywhere. At his mother's urging, he joined a socialist Zionist youth group. The leaders inspired him. "When I heard them speak, I became destined for that world I would never abandon—a world that at times took the form of Zionism, at times the struggle for human rights, at times the fight for freedom of expression," said Jacobo.

Jacobo became a journalist, committed to printing the truth, no matter what. Many Argentinians, including most Jewish leaders, were afraid to talk about the *desaparecidos*. This made Jacobo angry and determined. When he got death threats and his friends urged him to flee the country, he refused. Comparing himself to ancient Jews who stood up to the Romans, Jacobo said, "I am one who belongs to the Masada."

One morning, 20 police officers broke into Jacobo's home and arrested him. He was put in prison for 30 months and tortured while he was there. Human rights groups and world leaders demanded his freedom. Finally, he was released. He went into exile in Israel. There he wrote a memoir, *Prisoner Without a Name, Cell Without a Number*. When the military dictatorship in Argentina fell and democracy was restored, Jacobo returned to Argentina. He testified against his torturers. The worst offender received 25 years in prison.

Jacobo recounted the story of his imprisonment to many people. Some reacted with anger, others with resolve, still others with sympathy. Of all the reactions, Jacobo said, "The word that I hate most is 'unbelievable.'"

Jacobo Timerman escaped antisemitism in Europe by going to Argentina. So did . . .

Miguel Najdorf

Renowned Chess Grandmaster, 1910–1997

Mikel laughed silently to himself. *What a delight!* Not only had Mikel just won the 1936 Munich Chess Olympiad, now a Nazi official needed to present a gold medal to him, a Jew from Warsaw. Mikel didn't mind making things uncomfortable for the Nazi. *It served him right!* Watching the Nazi party come to power in Germany had caused plenty of fear and dread in Poland. Mikel almost hadn't attended the Munich Olympiad to protest Nazi antisemitism, but his coach convinced him to go to show his Polish pride. "I am a Pole of the Jewish religion," Mikel said proudly.

Three years after Munich, Mikel represented Poland at the Chess Olympiad in Buenos Aires, Argentina. His wife, Genia, and his daughter, Lusia, had planned to travel with him but, at the last minute, Genia got sick, so Mikel went alone. During the Olympiad, Germany invaded Poland. Mikel was playing chess when he heard the news. He was so upset that he forfeited the game. After the Olympiad, Mikel stayed in Argentina and tried tirelessly, and unsuccessfully, to get Genia and Lusia out of Poland. They died in Auschwitz. Mikel also lost his parents, four siblings, and nearly 200 other relatives in the Holocaust. When asked how he survived such a loss, Mikel said, "Chess helped me. Chess teaches one to lose."

Mikel became a citizen of Argentina, changing his name to Miguel. After the war, Miguel traveled to Poland to search for family members who may have survived, but he didn't find anyone. Years later, Miguel saw a man reading a Polish newspaper on a New York City subway. The man turned out to be his only surviving cousin.

Miguel remarried. He and his wife had two daughters. In his lifetime, Miguel won 52 international chess tournaments and earned the title of grandmaster. He was crowned Argentina's national chess champion seven times. He offered chess strategy to Pope John Paul II and played world leaders, including Fidel Castro, Winston Churchill, and the Shah of Iran. He even has a chess move, the Najdorf Defense, named in his honor. "When I start to play, I feel emotions, the desire to win, happiness. The beauty of chess is like nothing else," said Miguel.

Miguel Najdorf changed his name when he left Europe. So did . . .

David Ben-Gurion

First Prime Minister of Israel, 1886-1973

At 4:00 p.m. on May 14, 1948, David's black sedan pulled up to the Tel Aviv Museum. Half the city was gathered outside. David marched up the stairs and into a reception hall decorated in blue and white. Standing under a portrait of Zionist founder Theodor Herzl, David declared, "We, members of the People's Council, representatives of the Jewish community of Eretz Yisrael and the Zionist movement . . . hereby declare the establishment of a Jewish state in Eretz-Israel, to be known as the State of Israel."

With David's words, the modern State of Israel was born.

David was born in Plonsk, Poland. His father was a Zionist, a supporter of a Jewish homeland in the land of Israel. By the time David was a teenager, he had already founded a Zionist youth group called Ezra. When he was 20 years old, David left Poland for the land of Israel. He changed his last name from the Polish "Gruen" or "Green" to "Ben-Gurion," or "lion's son." A born organizer, David formed an early kibbutz and also the first Jewish defense group, called *HaShomer*, or the "The Guard."

During World War I, the Turkish authorities, who then ruled the land of Israel, grew concerned about David's growing influence. They exiled him, forcing him to leave the land of Israel. David went to the United States to raise awareness and money for the Labor Zionist cause. There, he met and married his wife, Paula. In 1917, when the British issued the Balfour Declaration supporting a Jewish homeland, David volunteered for the Jewish legion of the British Army. In 1920, once the British took control of the land of Israel, David returned.

While he was eager to declare statehood, David waited until a young Jewish state could survive. For well over a decade, David focused his energies on creating the foundation for a strong country in the future. He organized a powerful trade union called the *Histadrut* and a labor Zionist political party called *Mapai*.

In 1947, the United Nations voted to partition British Mandate Palestine, allowing for a Jewish state. David was ready. A visionary and pragmatist, beloved and criticized, David served as Israel's first prime minister, shepherding Israel through its infancy and supporting its initial struggles for existence.

David Ben-Gurion was Israel's first prime minister.
Who was the fifth?

Yitzhak Rabin

Israeli Soldier, Prime Minister & Peacemaker, 1922–1995

Yitzhak stood tensely on the White House lawn, waiting for the ceremony to begin. The year was 1993. Prime Minister of Israel, Yitzhak had come to Washington, DC, for the signing of the Oslo Accords. This peace treaty between Israel and the Palestinians was nothing short of miraculous. After a half century of bitter fighting, Israelis and Palestinians had agreed to put down their weapons.

Yitzhak had been a soldier for most of his life. He first held a gun when he was 16 years old and Israel wasn't yet a country. After school each day, Yitzhak went to a secret training class where he learned about pistols and military tactics. Yitzhak was fierce and relentless. He fought in Israel's War of Independence in 1948 and, over the next 20 years, every other major Israeli conflict. A military hero, Yitzhak was elected Israel's prime minister in 1974, promising to protect Israel with military strength.

But in the years that followed, a slow change overtook Yitzhak. He came to believe that endless fighting would not resolve the conflict between Palestinians and Israelis. The violence was making things worse. Perhaps peace would be the best way to protect Israel. In 1992, Yitzhak ran for prime minister again—but this time with a focus on peace. Because Yitzhak was a soldier, Israelis trusted him to make peace. Yitzhak won the election and immediately began peace talks.

Now Yitzhak stood on the White House lawn. His longtime enemy, Yasser Arafat, leader of the Palestine Liberation Organization, stood nearby. The Oslo Accords turned control of parts of the West Bank and the Gaza Strip over to the Palestinians and created a road map to a future Palestinian state. After signing, Yitzhak declared, "We who have fought against you, the Palestinians, we say to you today, in a loud and a clear voice: Enough of blood and tears. Enough!"

But not everybody agreed. On November 4, 1995, Yitzhak spoke at a peace rally in Tel Aviv. A right-wing, Jewish zealot shot Yitzhak in the back, killing him. Some worry the peace process died with Yitzhak, but his dream of peace lives on, providing hope and inspiration to those who see peace as a real possibility.

Yitzhak Rabin believed in the Israeli peace movement.
So does . . .

Edward Kessler

Interfaith Relations Thought Leader, 1963–

Growing up in London, England, Edward heard the story of his family's survival and resilience during World War II many times. Before the war, his family owned a successful business in Vienna, Austria, manufacturing umbrellas and walking sticks. His grandfather and father built the business, but then the Nazis destroyed it along with so many other things. When Edward's father came to England as a refugee, he made it his life's work to rebuild the family business. Naturally, his father assumed that when Edward and his brothers grew up, they would join the business and continue the family legacy. Edward tried, but he had other career interests too compelling to ignore. "Leaving the family business was the most difficult choice I've ever made. . . . I felt I was letting [my father] and my two brothers down," says Edward.

Edward was drawn to theology, the study of religion. He wanted to make it his life's work. Edward studied first at Harvard University and earned his doctorate in religion at Cambridge University. He credits a Latin teacher with sparking his academic success: "He gave me confidence in my own ability. That's a huge thing when it comes from outside the family, and I'm indebted to him forever."

At Cambridge, Edward focused on the connections between Judaism, Christianity, and Islam and how to manage conflict that results from their differences. In 1998, he founded a center for interfaith studies, now known as the Woolf Institute. Edward outlines four steps for interfaith understanding: encounter people who are different, find what you have in common, try to understand others as they wish to be understood, and build up confidence in who you are. "I'm quite optimistic: there's been a huge shift in understanding between Jews and Christians in the past 40 or 50 years . . . almost unthinkable to my parents' generation," says Edward.

Edward believes political leaders should be trained in religion and belief. He has worked with leaders in Israel, the Palestinian Authority, and Jordan to address conflicts over sacred space in Jerusalem. On a more local level, Edward talks with police, teachers, and prison officers about faith issues, so they can better understand their diverse communities.

Edward has a nightly ritual: "I have a simple, personal prayer at night before I go to sleep: for my family, and the community in which I live, and a little prayer for the whole world."

Edward Kessler considers trusting relationships vital.
So did . . .

Eddie Jacobson

Best Friends with a President, 1891-1955

Eddie was completely and utterly ordinary. He wasn't a great scholar. In fact, he only finished 8th grade. He wasn't a stellar athlete. He had no real musical talent. But Eddie did have one exceptional trait. He was a loyal friend. What's more: Eddie's oldest friend happened to be President Harry Truman.

Eddie and Harry grew up together in Kansas City and served in the Army together. Harry became a US senator, then vice president, then president. Eddie stayed in Kansas City and sold clothes. He sent care packages to the White House with shirts, ties, and even underwear.

Eddie had one cardinal rule for friendship, especially when it came to Harry: He never requested favors. Friends would press Eddie to ask Harry for special treatment. Eddie told them, "In my thirty-seven years of friendship with President Truman, I have never asked a favor of him."

Eddie was a good friend but also a proud Jew. In the spring of 1948, the State of Israel was preparing to declare its independence. But Harry Truman was tired of hearing about Israel and hadn't agreed to recognize Israel as a country. Jewish leaders came to Eddie: would he speak to Harry and ask him to support Israel? The future of the Jewish state might hinge on this favor. Eddie had a choice. He could preserve his cardinal rule of friendship. Or he could support the new Jewish state.

Eddie thought about the Holocaust, its trauma just a few years old. He thought about Israel, not yet a country and yet on the brink of war. Eddie made his decision. He went to Washington. But as soon as Eddie arrived at the White House, Harry said, "I know what you are here for, and the answer is no."

But Eddie wouldn't give up. He told Harry all the reasons why Israel needed to exist. Still, Harry wouldn't promise to recognize Israel.

On May 14, 1948, Israel declared its independence. Like Jews around the world, Eddie sat by his radio, waiting to hear what Harry would do. Eleven minutes passed. The wait was excruciating. Finally, Harry announced, "As President of the United States, I hereby recognize the new Jewish state of Israel."

At that moment, Eddie, ordinary in every way, knew the extraordinary power of friendship.

Eddie Jacobson sold clothes for a living. So does . . .

Isaac Mizrahi

Self-Made Fashion Designer, 1961–

When Isaac was 10, his father gave him a special gift. A bicycle? A skateboard? His own record player? No—a sewing machine. Isaac's father worked in the garment industry and hoped that Isaac would someday join the family business. "I have to say that my father's business didn't appeal to me, but of course, the sewing machines and the craft of making clothes did," says Isaac. He used the sewing machine to sew a High Holiday outfit for his mother, his first foray into fashion.

As a boy, Isaac didn't quite fit in. He grew up in the Flatbush neighborhood of Brooklyn, New York, in a close-knit community of Jews from Syria. At the Yeshivah of Flatbush, Isaac often clashed with the administrators, who didn't appreciate his creativity. It didn't help that Isaac drew fashion designs in the margins of his Hebrew books. "I was effeminate and artistic, and I was bullied and ridiculed for it," says Isaac.

A teacher convinced his parents to let him audition for the High School for the Performing Arts in Manhattan. There, Isaac thrived. He came out as gay to his friends, but not his parents. After graduation, Isaac went to the Parsons School of Design. He had an internship with Perry Ellis and his first job was with Calvin Klein. Eventually, Isaac opened his own design company. His style was youthful, sophisticated, and bright. Soon, the Isaac Mizrahi line was available at all the finest stores, including Neiman Marcus, Saks Fifth Avenue, and Bloomingdale's.

When financial troubles forced Isaac to close his business, he reinvented himself as an entertainer. He hosted a talk show, acted in a one-man show about his life and appeared on television and in the movies. Then the store Target contacted him. Isaac was hesitant to partner with a discount store, but he gave it a try. The partnership proved extremely lucrative, with over $300 million in sales each year.

Today, Isaac is a boundary-breaking, influential designer. But his story began as a creative young boy at odds with the traditional community around him. Isaac says he is "an artist first and a Jew fifth." Still, the Jewish Museum in New York created an exhibit of his Jewish influences, including a jumpsuit with an oversized Jewish star belt buckle. Isaac says, "If crosses are everywhere, why not make the Star of David ubiquitous too?"

Isaac Mizrahi built a business empire from nothing. So did . . .

32
24
16
31
30
29
28

Jennie Grossinger

Resort Owner Committed to Integration, 1892-1972

Seven-year-old Jennie hugged her father good-bye. He was leaving their poor farming village in Austria and going to New York City. "As soon as I make enough money, I'll send for you," he promised.

It took three long years, but finally, her father sent steamship tickets for Jennie, her mother, and her sister. When they got to Ellis Island, Jennie couldn't speak a word of English. At school on the Lower East Side, Jennie was put in first grade even though she was 10 years old. Still, she struggled. At age 13, Jennie quit school so she could work to help support her family. For 10 hours a day, she worked in the same sweatshop as her father, sewing buttonholes on clothes. If she made even the smallest mistake, the foreman told her to start over. In her first week working, she earned $1.50.

Missing life in the country and tired of sweatshops, Jennie's father scraped together enough money to buy a farm in the Catskill Mountains. But the rocky land was nearly impossible to farm. Determined not to let her family fail, Jennie started renting guest rooms in their farmhouse. When Jennie got married, her husband stayed in New York City and sent guests to the farm. He would encourage visitors by promising an affordable country retreat with kosher food. The house didn't have electricity, heat, or indoor plumbing, but Jennie's warm and welcoming personality and her mother's excellent cooking made it a success.

In time, Grossinger's Resort expanded to 35 buildings over 1,200 acres. It had crystal chandeliers, a stable, pools, tennis courts, a golf course, and even an airstrip. In its heyday after World War II, Grossinger's hosted 150,000 guests each year. The most popular entertainers of the day played there. Many resorts didn't allow Jewish or African American guests. Grossinger's became the "it" place for Jews on the East Coast. Jennie welcomed everybody, regardless of race. Jennie extended a special invitation to Jackie Robinson, the first African American to play Major League Baseball. They became close friends. Soon prominent people who were not Jewish—like the Roosevelts, Kennedys, and Rockefellers—started vacationing at the resort.

After Jennie turned the resort over to her children, she lived in a cottage on the grounds and still greeted guests. The girl who sewed buttonholes to survive had become the most famous hotelkeeper in the world.

Jennie Grossinger racially integrated her resort.
Who did the same for basketball?

YOUR HOSTESS

Red Auerbach

Basketball Coaching Legend, 1917–2006

Marie and Hyman Auerbach, deli owners in Brooklyn, New York, named their infant son "Arnold." But the name did not stick. Arnold had flaming red hair and a fiery personality to match. Soon, everybody just called him "Red."

For Jewish city kids like Red, basketball was *the* sport in the 1920s. "There was no football, no baseball," said Red. "They were too expensive." So many young Jews played basketball that the term "Jew ball" was coined to describe their playing style: active teamwork, quick passing, and strong defense. Red used his basketball talent to get into college, earning a scholarship to George Washington University.

In 1950, Red became coach of the Boston Celtics. Fifteen years later, he was promoted to general manager, then team president. Under Red's leadership, the Celtics won 16 national championships. He coached 938 winning games with the Celtics, the most of any NBA coach. But Red held another record: the NBA coach expelled from the most games for arguing with referees. Red also loved to taunt the opposing team. If the Celtics were ahead, Red would smugly light up a victory cigar before the game was even over.

With his players, Red was warm but demanding. Red had a particular talent in drafting, signing, and trading players. He had an uncanny ability to look ahead and predict a player's potential. Sometimes, Red made trade or draft choices that seemed illogical. But a season or two later, his reasoning became clear. "I don't believe in statistics. There are too many factors that can't be measured. You can't measure a ballplayer's heart," said Red.

Red is credited with helping to break basketball's color barrier. In 1950, his first year as Celtics coach, Red drafted Chuck Cooper, the first African American player ever chosen in an NBA draft. And when Red moved from coach to general manager, he named Bill Russell as his successor—the first African American to coach a major professional sports team. Red believed that integrating basketball was the right thing to do. But he also knew it would help win games. Signing players based on talent rather than race simply made competitive sense.

Red coached some of basketball's greatest players and helped some average players become great. His advice: "Take pride in what you do. The kind of pride I'm talking about is not the arrogant puffed-up kind; it's just the whole idea of caring—fiercely caring."

Red Auerbach led the Celtics to nine NBA championships.
Who won multiple WNBA championships?

Sue Bird

WNBA Basketball Star, 1980-

A thunderous cheer filled Madison Square Garden as the New York Knicks took to the arena floor. A six-year-old named Sue sat in the stands, mesmerized by the game. She watched as the players leapt toward the basket, making shots that seemed to defy gravity. She had never been to a professional basketball game before. Could she do this, too?

Sue went home and shot baskets in her driveway for countless hours. Her parents told her if she trained hard, she could succeed at anything. Her high school basketball coach told her, "Do you want to be a player who had great potential, or do you want to be that player that reached her potential?"

Sue wanted to reach her potential. But she also knew the reality. Her potential was limited. She couldn't be a professional basketball player, at least not in the United States. Not as a girl. There was no professional league for her. During her senior year of high school, something game-changing happened: the Women's National Basketball Association (WNBA) was formed. Sue could work hard at college ball and be drafted as a professional basketball player.

Sue was the number one pick in the 2002 WNBA draft. For two decades, Sue played for the Seattle Storm, helping them win four WNBA championships. She won 10 Olympic and World Cup medals, more than any other basketball player in history—woman or man. But Sue still faced gender inequity. WNBA players earn much less than NBA players. Sue played in Europe in the off season to earn more money. Since Israel belongs to the European league, Sue became an Israeli citizen in 2006 to expand her playing options.

At the 2016 Rio Olympics, Sue met soccer star Megan Rapinoe. Sue and Megan quickly became a couple and, after four years, they got engaged. Sue had never been public about being a lesbian, considering it private and not related to basketball. With Megan's encouragement, Sue has publicly celebrated their relationship, striving to be a role model for other lesbian athletes.

These days, Sue and Megan use their star power to advocate for social issues like the Black Lives Matter and Say Her Name movements. They fight for equal pay and more press coverage for women athletes. Together, Sue and Megan have won more medals and championships than perhaps any other couple in sports—a power couple working together toward change.

Sue Bird advocates for pay equity for women.
Pay equity has also been an important goal for . . .

USA
6
molten

Janet Yellen

Secretary of the Treasury, 1946–

In the working-class neighborhood of Brooklyn, New York, a young girl named Janet talked with her father's patients as they waited to be seen. Her father, a family physician, had his medical office on the first floor of their house. She heard stories about struggling to make ends meet, about jobs lost, and hard work for low wages. Janet wished she knew how to help them.

Her parents had stories to share, too. They had grown up during the Great Depression and watched their families struggle. Her father's family had emigrated from a Polish village later destroyed in the Holocaust. More culturally Jewish than religious, Janet's parents taught her to study hard and make a difference in the world.

Janet excelled at school. At Fort Hamilton High School, Janet edited the school newspaper and joined the pep squad. Her senior year, she was voted a "class celebrity" and graduated valedictorian.

Janet went to Brown University, where she took her first economics class. She loved economics from the moment she started studying it. She had found her passion. Janet went on to Yale for graduate studies. She graduated with her PhD in Economics in 1971, the only woman among two dozen students in her department.

She taught at Harvard from 1971-1976, one of only two female professors in the economics department. Then she went to work at the Federal Reserve Board in Washington, DC, the central bank that sets economic policy in the United States. She met her husband, George Akerlof, a Nobel-Prize-winning economist, in the bank's cafeteria. They have one son; he also became an economist.

President Bill Clinton nominated Janet to chair his Council of Economic Advisors. President Barack Obama asked Janet to chair the Federal Reserve Board. And, in 2020, President Joe Biden nominated her to be Secretary of the Treasury. She was the first woman to hold any of these positions and the first person to hold all three. Like Alexander Hamilton, the first Secretary of the Treasury, Janet Yellen even has a rap song written about her.

Janet's greatest passion is using her economic knowledge to help everyday Americans. At her confirmation hearing to become Treasury Secretary, Janet said, "We must restore the American dream—a society where each person can rise to their potential and dream even bigger for their children. As Treasury Secretary, I will work every day towards rebuilding that dream for all."

Janet Yellen watched her father's patients struggle to afford medical care. Who had a similar experience?

THIS NOTE IS LEGAL TENDER
FOR ALL DEBTS, PUBLIC AND
12
DOLLARS

Danny Siegel

Educator, Poet & Tzedakah Hero, 1944-

As a boy, Danny often went on house calls with his father, a country doctor in Virginia. "I witnessed the kind of people he treated: kind people, simple people, people who would give you the shirt off their back, bring you in and feed you if you were hungry," says Danny. These simple kindnesses made an impression on Danny, instilling in him a passion to help others.

In high school, Danny's life revolved around United Synagogue Youth (USY), the Conservative Jewish youth movement. Danny served as chapter president, regional president, and then international president. Because USY meant so much to him, Danny helped it thrive long after his teen years. Danny staffed USY's trips to Israel and served as their tzedakah (charity) coordinator. There is a Jewish custom of giving tzedakah money to a person traveling to Israel, so they can give it to a needy person or cause when they arrive. Having a good deed to complete is said to ensure a safe journey. Danny built on this custom. In 1975, Danny raised $955 to give out in Israel. The next year, he raised $1,600, then $6,000 the year after that, and then $12,000 the year after that. In 1981, Danny established the Ziv Tzedakah Fund. Between 1981 and 2008, Danny raised $12 million for the Ziv Fund, mostly through very small donations. He gave the money to "Mitzvah Heroes" in Israel, people like Hadassah Levi, who rescued abandoned babies with Down syndrome and Myriam Mendilow, who helped Jerusalem's poor, elderly residents find new purpose.

Danny's mission became to inspire as many people as possible to learn Jewishly and do good deeds. He bought a Winnebago RV and set out across the United States. Danny visited more than 500 American cities! He sought out Jewish communities, brought them books, did original poetry readings, and shared a message of giving.

Danny's message is clear: with very little effort, everybody is capable of making a difference in another person's life. Inspired? Then follow Danny's advice. He says to ask yourself, "What am I good at? What do I like to do? And what's bothering me about the world today?" Then use the answers to these questions to go out and make a difference.

Danny has been called the "Mitzvah Maniac" and the "Pied Piper of Tzedakah". He believes that heroes exist everywhere, performing small acts of kindness with big results. Although Danny would not admit it, he is one of those heroes.

Danny Siegel studied at the Jewish Theological Seminary of America. So did . . .

Amichai Lau-Lavie

Rabbi, Organizer & Performance Artist, 1969-

As a boy in Israel, Amichai could trace his family back through 39 generations of rabbis. Far back, his ancestors were rabbis in Eastern Europe. During his childhood, his relatives were prominent rabbis in Israel. His uncle and his cousin eventually both served as the Chief Rabbi of Israel. Born into a rabbinic dynasty, Amichai lived an Orthodox Jewish life. But something just didn't feel right.

When Amichai became bar mitzvah, it all came together for him. His Torah portion included verses traditionally interpreted to condemn homosexuality. By then, Amichai knew he was gay but hadn't told anyone. So chanting his Torah portion proved very difficult. He yearned to live Jewishly and be authentic to his identity. Becoming a rabbi, like so many of his relatives and ancestors, did not seem like a possibility.

In high school, Amichai discovered drama and theater. After serving as a paratrooper and medic in the Israeli army, Amichai found his way to New York City and founded Storahtelling, a dramatic project that explores Jewish texts through performance and stagecraft. He even developed his own motivational comedy act, appearing as "Rebbetzin Hadassah Gross"—the widow of six prominent rabbis.

As time passed, Amichai began to feel the family calling to be a rabbi. After focusing for so long on Jewish stories and drama, he wanted to delve more deeply into Jewish law and how it applied to modern Jewish life. Amichai enrolled in the Jewish Theological Seminary (JTS), a rabbinical school for the Conservative movement of Judaism. Extremely important to Amichai, JTS accepts openly gay and lesbian students. "I like how Conservative Judaism straddles halacha and innovation. Jewish law has a vote, but not a veto," he says.

While still a rabbinical student in New York, Amichai founded the Lab/Shul, a Jewish community welcoming to everybody, regardless of religion, race, nationality, or gender orientation. Recalling the discomfort he felt at his own bar mitzvah, Amichai focused on redefining b'nai mitzvah. He calls it B Mitzvah. He also strives to be inclusive for interfaith families. "I know what it's like to be ostracized and to be partially welcomed," he says. "I know what it's like to hop between identities, to be hyphenated."

Nowadays, Amichai is often included on lists of the most inspiring and influential Jewish leaders. *The New York Times* even called him a "rock star."

Amichai Lau-Lavie was born into a rabbinic dynasty.
So was . . .

Abby Stein

Rabbi & Transgender Activist, 1991–

Abby slipped into the mall bathroom, carefully hiding a borrowed tablet. Like any Viznitz Hasidic man, Abby had a beard and wore a black suit and hat. The Viznitz Hasidim largely keep to themselves, rarely use the internet, and speak only Yiddish, even in Brooklyn where Abby was raised. As a rabbi in his community, Abby couldn't sit in the middle of the mall using a tablet. In the bathroom, Abby nervously typed "Can a boy turn into a girl?" into the search engine. Abby read the very first entry: "transgender." At age 20, she finally had a word to describe herself. She broke down in tears.

For as long as Abby could remember, everybody considered her to be a boy. She went to the boy's yeshiva and celebrated a bar mitzvah. But despite it all, when Abby looked in the mirror, she saw a girl. As a young child, she even composed a blessing asking for a girl's body. She repeated these words each night before bed: "Holy creator, I am going to sleep now, and I look like a boy. I am begging you, when I wake up in the morning, I want to be a girl."

Learning the word "transgender," Abby finally realized she was not alone. But if she wanted to live as a transgender woman, she would need to leave the close-knit Hasidic community that had been her only home. She would be shunned, perhaps even by her own family. Despite it all, Abby was determined to live as a woman. When Abby came out as a transgender woman, her parents painfully cut off contact. But Abby had a new joy about her. Living outside the Hasidic community, she started much of life again—learning English, studying secular subjects for the first time, and making friends of all different backgrounds.

These days, Abby has reclaimed her title as rabbi but in the liberal Jewish community. She helped to establish a support group for transgender people who grew up Orthodox, wrote a memoir, and has spoken around the world—often on college campuses—about her personal experience. She is also an activist for immigration reform, women's rights, racial equality, and many other causes.

"I like to shake things up. . . . It's a way of changing things. Making trouble is actually helping," says Abby.

Abby Stein stands up for transgender rights and inclusion.
So does . . .

Daniel Radcliffe

Actor & Activist, Living with a Disability, 1989–

For fans around the globe, the Harry Potter movies opened up a whole magical world of wizardry: house elves, quidditch, goblins, dragons, horcruxes, mandrakes. For Daniel, the series' star, the Harry Potter movies opened up his world, but in a different way. "I was at a private school—an almost exclusively white, very privileged place—and I was put into a film set with people from 100 different backgrounds, races, classes, everything. Suddenly, because of Potter, my worldview got much wider than it would have been," says Daniel.

Before his magical movie stardom, Daniel got his start acting in the role of a monkey in the school play. Daniel was shy, often bullied in school, and a little clumsy due to a neurological disorder called dyspraxia that makes tasks like tying shoes and neat handwriting difficult. Daniel gives this advice to kids with similar challenges: "Do not let it stop you. It has never held me back, and some of the smartest people I know are people who have learning disabilities. The fact that some things are more of a struggle will only make you more determined, harder working and more imaginative in the solutions you find to problems."

Dyspraxia is only one of the reasons that Daniel felt different from his classmates. Daniel's mother is a South African Jew and his father is an Irish Protestant. He considers himself Jewish and Irish, although he is English. "I've always had an awareness and pride about those two cultures and histories. And I always felt a little bit different from most people around me," says Daniel.

Not a religious person, Daniel's Jewish identity developed from ethnic pride and family history, especially how his ancestors overcame antisemitism. Today, Daniel is a vocal advocate for diversity, championing religious tolerance and supporting LGBTQ youth. "You don't have to be gay to be a supporter, you just have to be human," says Daniel.

Since Harry Potter, Daniel has chosen to do an eclectic mix of movies and plays—musicals, political dramas, love stories, and even horror movies. A shy, awkward schoolboy no more, Daniel says, "There is something inherently valuable about being a misfit. It's not to say that every person who has artistic talent was a social outcast, but there is definitely a value for identifying yourself differently and being proud that you are different."

Daniel Radcliffe has learned to compensate for a disability. So has . . .

Rebecca Dubowe

Rabbinic Leader with Hearing Loss, 1962–

When Rebecca was a baby in Los Angeles, her parents noticed something worrisome. She didn't respond to the melody from her music box. At 22 months, Rebecca was diagnosed as deaf. "My parents cried a little bit, and then they got busy," Rebecca says. "They treated me like any other child. I did everything a child has the right to do. They took me to school, to the philharmonic, to the library."

While many deaf children learn American Sign Language as their primary language, Rebecca's parents focused on teaching her to read lips and speak. She would live in a hearing world. "My first language is English, my second is Hebrew, and my third is ASL (American Sign Language)," Rebecca says. "They're all equally beautiful and expressive."

Acceptance wasn't always easy. Rebecca's parents were her fiercest advocates. Rebecca herself needed to have grit and determination. Several public elementary schools refused to admit her. A Jewish day school accepted her on a six-month trial. The administrators assumed she wouldn't succeed. Of course, Rebecca proved them wrong. For her bat mitzvah, Rebecca insisted on chanting her haftarah. And, as a teenager, Rebecca fought her high school principal to attend honors classes.

On the first day of college, Rebecca met her future husband, Michael Dubowe, in the college bookstore. Michael was also deaf, also relied on reading lips rather than sign language, and also was a Reform Jew. Rebecca asked him out and they immediately clicked. They learned sign language together in college.

Hebrew Union College-Jewish Institute of Religion, the Reform rabbinical seminary, hesitated before accepting Rebecca. They hadn't had a deaf student before. Both the school and Rebecca pledged to be patient with one another. The school provided interpreters for all her classes, which came in most handy with heavily bearded professors whose lips were hard to read. Since ordination, Rebecca has served congregations in California, Illinois, and New Jersey. She makes simple accommodations, like passing out printed copies of her sermons, to make sure she is understood.

Rebecca is an energetic advocate for inclusion in synagogue life. She has toured the country with her story and message. "I don't consider myself as having a disability; I believe we all have different abilities," she says. "We were all created *b'tzelem Elokim*—in God's image—and we are all unique."

In school, Rebecca Dubowe had to advocate for herself to be treated fairly. So did . . .

Alma Hernandez

State Legislator, 1993–

Alma liked the ring of her new Jewish name: Malka Librada. A Hebrew-Spanish name roughly translated as "queen of freedom." It was perfect for her, a Jewish-Latina committed to social justice. While her grandfather in Mexico had been Jewish, Alma formally converted, to make her identity official. She expected a small celebration at her naming. One hundred people showed up. Her family liked to throw big parties—it was the Mexican way.

But Alma's ethnic identity had not always been so simple or joyful. Alma went to a high school in Tucson, Arizona, which sometimes had strained race relations and a system biased against students of color. An honors student, Alma stayed out of trouble. Then one afternoon, Alma saw two older girls taunting her sister Consuela for being Mexican. When Alma stood up for Consuela, the girls attacked her. A school resource officer assumed Alma instigated the fight and threw her to the ground, permanently injuring her spine. Alma was kicked out of school and sent to a juvenile detention center. She worried she would be there for a long time. But her parents worked hard to prove that she was innocent.

Some people let such experiences negatively define them. Not Alma. Alma's experiences directed her into politics. She started as a campaign volunteer as a teenager. Then she ran for office herself and won, becoming the youngest woman elected to Arizona's legislature and the first Jewish Latina elected to such a position in the United States. Now she can change the way kids are treated and help pass laws to protect those who are attacked for no reason other than their ethnicity. "I don't want anyone else to have to go through what I went through," she says.

Alma embraces all parts of her identity with boundless energy. She is an avid supporter of Israel. She advocated to make Holocaust education mandatory in Arizona. She has stood up to antisemites online. She founded Tucson Jews for Justice to help migrants on the border. Alma says, "We're all human. We're neighbors. And as Jews, we know what it is like to be immigrants. So it's our duty to do what we can to welcome others who come here."

Many days, Alma wears a golden charm around her neck with "Malka" written in Hebrew—her small reminder to be a leader for freedom.

Alma Hernandez blends her Latin American and Jewish heritages. So did . . .

Moacyr Scliar

Brazilian Physician & Writer, 1937–2011

A person's name often has a story. Sometimes a name honors the memory of a close relative, sometimes a name honors a belief or value, and sometimes a name honors a place or role model. When Moacyr was born, his parents didn't choose a name in Yiddish, their native language, or Portuguese, the language that they spoke daily. Rather "Moacyr" is a name in Tupi, an indigenous Brazilian language, and a well-known character in Brazilian literature. After emigrating from Russia, Moacyr's parents found a good home in Brazil and wanted to honor it. Moacyr grew up in the Jewish quarter of Porto Alegre, a city in the south of Brazil. He attended both Yiddish and Roman Catholic schools. He was active in a Zionist youth group and also completely at home exploring the streets of Porto Alegre. Since Brazil had limited antisemitism and racism, Moacyr felt comfortable with his dual identities.

Moacyr trained as a physician but also felt the pull to write. While working as a doctor, Moacyr wrote and published over 70 books for adults, young adults, and children. His books were translated from Portuguese into a dozen languages. In most of his books, Moacyr explored growing up Jewish in Brazil. Moacyr melded Jewish humor, Latin American culture, and fantasy when writing. "We have this double identity—the identity from our parents and the identity of the country we live in. To have a double identity can be a problem, but not for writers. For writers it is a source of inspiration," says Moacyr.

Perhaps Moacyr's best known novel is *The Centaur in the Garden*—about a Jewish centaur, a half-human and half-horse, born to immigrant parents. "The centaur is a symbol of the double identity. . . . At home, you speak Yiddish, eat gefilte fish, and celebrate Shabbat. But in the streets, you have soccer, samba, and Portuguese. After a while you feel like a centaur," says Moacyr. To this day, Brazilian teachers regularly assign *The Centaur in the Garden* as class reading. The National Yiddish Book Center calls it one of the 100 most important modern Jewish novels.

Moacyr embraced all his identities: Brazilian and Jewish, physician and writer, husband and father. He encouraged his readers to celebrate their complex selves. He said, "I think that you are entitled to all the identities you happen to have. You have the right to several identities."

Moacyr Scliar wrote about relationships and identity.
So did . . .

Ann Landers, 1918-2002
& Abigail Van Buren, 1918-2013

Twin Sisters, Competing Advice Columnists

Esther Pauline and Pauline Esther were born just 18 minutes apart in Sioux City, Iowa. Along with their matching names, the girls wore matching outfits and had matching interests. Their parents owned a movie and vaudeville theater. Esther and Pauline entertained the audiences by playing violin and singing Yiddish duets.

Esther and Pauline both studied journalism and psychology in college. That's when they started offering advice to others. They wrote a joint gossip column for the school newspaper. On their 21st birthday, they had a double wedding, complete with three rabbis, a bridal party of 22, and 700 guests. Of course, the twins wore matching dresses.

The two couples settled in Eau Claire, Wisconsin. There, the tight bond between the twins began to break. Pauline loved their matching lives, but Esther craved individuality. "She wanted to be the first violin in the school orchestra, but I was," said Pauline. "She swore she'd marry a millionaire, but I did."

In 1955, Ann Landers, the popular advice columnist at the *Chicago Sun-Times*, died. The newspaper ran a competition to find a writer for the column. Esther won! As the new Ann Landers, Esther received thousands of letters asking for advice on love, family, and marriage. Overwhelmed, Esther asked Pauline to help answer them. When the editors found out, they told Esther she couldn't have a co-author. By then, Pauline was hooked on writing. "My stuff was published—and it looked awfully good in print," said Pauline.

Soon after, Pauline and her husband moved to California and she became the advice columnist for the *San Francisco Chronicle*. Writing under the pen name Abigail Van Buren, she launched *Dear Abby*. Pauline's *Dear Abby* column had more sarcasm and one-liners while Esther's *Ask Ann Landers* went more in-depth. Pauline and Esther became fierce competitors, each vying to have her column printed in as many newspapers as possible. They stopped speaking to each other. Both columns were great successes, transforming Esther and Pauline into America's confidantes. *Ask Ann Landers* peaked at 90 million readers in 1,200 newspapers while *Dear Abby* peaked at 110 million readers in 1,400 newspapers, the most popular syndicated column of all time.

These twin girls, then women, had matching names, clothes, interests, and ambition. And for many years, their advice was what people looked for to start their day.

Ann Landers and Abigail Van Buren were twins.
Another twin is . . .

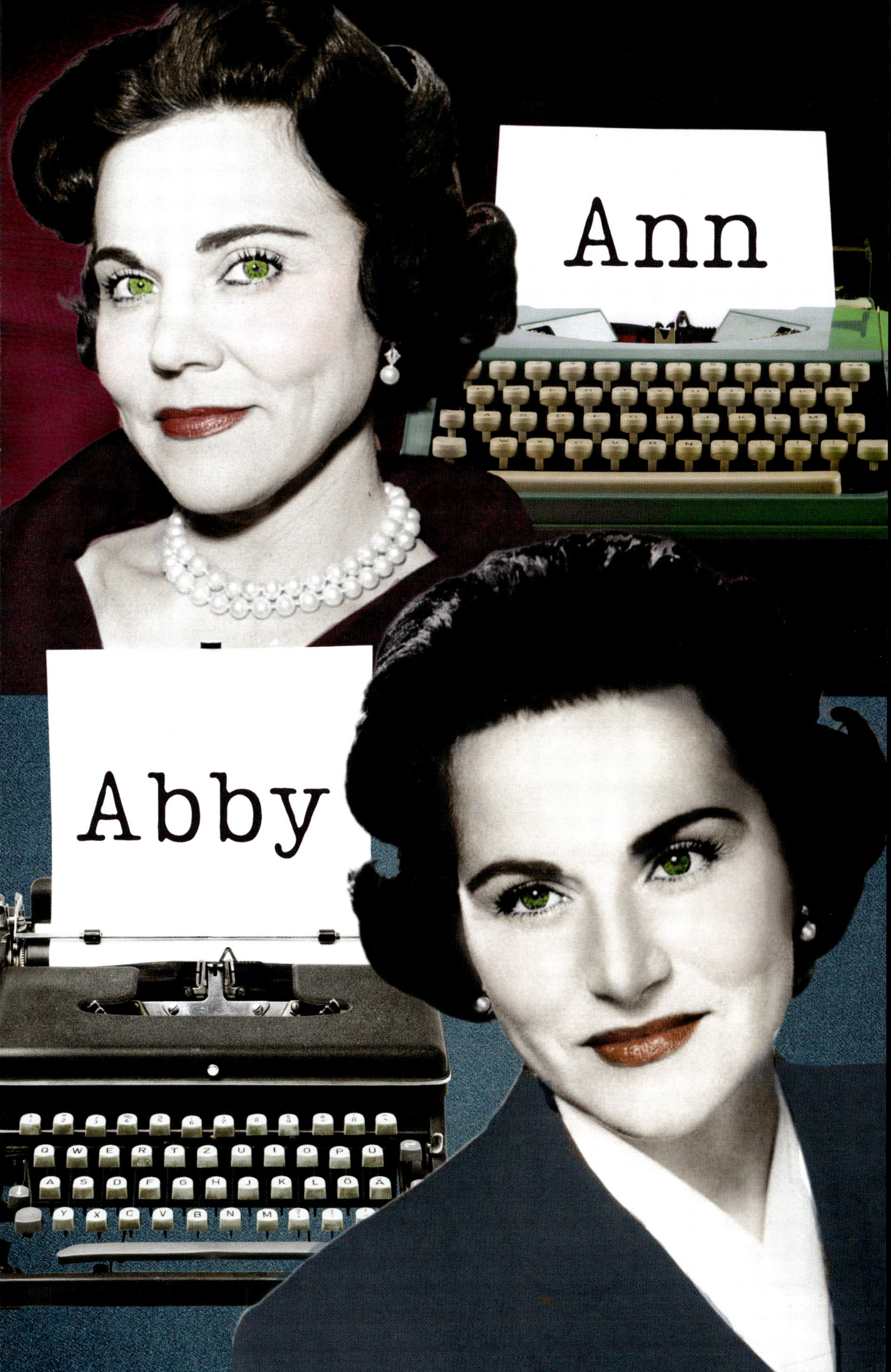
Ann
Abby

Becky Silverstein

Gender-Bending Rabbi & LGBTQ Activist, 1982-

Becky grew up in Great Neck, New York, part of a large, blended family. Becky's parents divorced when he was 10. Eventually both remarried. Becky has a twin sister and two other sisters, plus six half-sisters—all together, nine sisters and Becky. As a child, Becky always carried a sense of not really knowing where he belonged. "A sense of not feeling like a 'girl' and not quite being a 'boy,'" he says.

This uneasy sense continued through college. Although he met one or two transgender students while at Smith College, he didn't learn the language to describe himself as nonbinary until rabbinical school. Today, Becky identifies as genderqueer, meaning he does not fit into a neatly predefined category. Becky uses his birth name and the pronouns he/him/his. Are you confused? That is the point. He chose to use Becky along with male pronouns to make people think about gender and identity. Becky realizes his choice of pronouns might confuse some people. But he says, "It requires us to discover the place in our bodies and our minds where that threat exists, to name it, and to actively work to unseat it."

Becky studied engineering at Smith College. But by the end of college, he was clearly more interested in gathering the Jewish community than working in engineering. He was passionate about connecting with people and serving the greater good by being in relationship with people. He began studying to become a rabbi. Following his ordination, he became the first transgender rabbi engaged by a Conservative synagogue.

These days, Becky serves as a facilitator for a national organization named Keshet. Keshet means rainbow and its mission is working toward full LGBTQ equality in Jewish life. Becky also teaches Talmud to queer and trans Jews at SVARA: A Traditionally Radical Yeshiva. And Becky is the founder and rabbi of Beyn Kodesh l'Chol, an inclusive Jewish start-up community outside Boston.

Becky's approach to Judaism is finding those elements that have personal meaning and embracing them. He teaches his community, "Let's dig in and see where we get and what the tradition can offer us from a place that's affirming and embracing from a place that is about loving ourselves and creating a path for ourselves that is described in Jewish language."

Becky Silverstein studied engineering. So did . . .

Judith Love Cohen

NASA Engineer Dedicated to Girls in Science, 1933–2016

"Houston, we've had a problem here," called out Astronaut James Swigert from space on April 13, 1970. Two days after takeoff, an oxygen explosion damaged the Apollo 13 spacecraft. Swigert's and two other astronauts' lives were in danger. They might not make it home.

Back on earth, Judith and her team sprang into action. They had designed the Abort-Guidance System on the Apollo spacecraft's lunar module—basically a lifeboat if the spaceship was damaged. Their system guided the astronauts back to earth, saving their lives.

As a young girl in Brooklyn, Judith found astronomy fascinating, but she hadn't heard of any female astronomers. Since her math teacher was a woman, Judith decided to focus on math. By the time she was in fifth grade, her classmates were paying her to do their math homework. In most of these classes, she was the only girl. As a high school senior, Judith told her guidance counselor that she wanted to study math in college. The counselor responded, "I think you ought to go to a nice finishing school and learn to be a lady."

Thankfully, Judith did not listen to the counselor. She studied math, then engineering, in college. At the same time, she was a dancer in New York's famed Metropolitan Opera Ballet Company. Judith completed both an undergraduate and graduate degree in electrical engineering and never met another female engineering student.

In addition to the Apollo Space Program, Judith worked on the Minuteman missile and the Hubble Space Telescope, fulfilling her childhood dream of working in astronomy. When she retired, she launched a children's book company to encourage girls to pursue careers in science and engineering.

Judith was fully dedicated both to her family and her career. When she went into labor with her fourth child, she was in the middle of a vexing and important problem at work. She took a printout of the problem with her to the hospital. Later that day, she called her boss and told him that she had figured it out. And, yes, the baby had been born and was healthy. She and her husband Thomas Black named the baby Jack.

Jack Black—the comedian.

One Mother's Day, Jack posted a picture of Judith with one of her satellites and these words: "Judith Love Cohen. Aerospace engineer. Author of children's books. Loving mother of four."

Judith Love Cohen did research into the space sciences.
So did . . .

Arno Penzias

German Refugee & Nobel-winning Physicist, 1933-

Six-year-old Arno knew one word in English: "affidavit." Certainly it is not the first word most children learn, but an affidavit would prove lifesaving for Arno and his family. When Nazis took power in Germany, Arno's family became desperate to leave. A sensitive, alert boy, Arno overheard bits and pieces about the Nazis and could sense his parents' tension. "I began to realize that there were bad things that my parents couldn't completely control, something to do with being Jewish. I learned that everything would be fine if we could only get to 'America,'" says Arno.

But to get into the United States, his parents needed an affidavit—a form proving they had relatives in America and could financially support themselves. A friend of Arno's father, already in the U.S., claimed that they were cousins—which they were not. Arno and his brother left first. His parents placed their sons on the Kindertransport, a rescue effort that took 10,000 Jewish children to Great Britain. Most children on the Kindertransport never saw their parents again. Arno was lucky. His parents' affidavit was approved. The family reunited in Great Britain and left for the United States.

But life was not easy in America. His parents worked very hard so Arno could go to college. Arno thought he'd study chemistry but then took a class in physics. Discovering the mysteries of the universe fascinated him. He studied for many years and earned a PhD. Then Arno got a research position at Bell Laboratories, one of the leading technology research centers in the world.

Arno and another scientist used a special antenna built to measure radio waves emitted by gas surrounding the galaxy. But like the young boy overhearing his parents and sensing tension, Arno kept hearing a constant radio noise picked up by the antenna. Arno felt this noise pointed to something bigger. And he was right. This noise turned out to be cosmic background microwave radiation left over from the Big Bang and the creation of the universe. He had found remnants from the universe's birth! In 1978, Arno shared a Nobel Prize in Physics for his work.

Arno kept working, researching the universe for many years after most people retire. With his sensitive ear and alert mind, he kept making discoveries. Arno listened hard, thought deeply, and discovered evidence of the creation of the world.

Arno Penzias escaped Nazi Germany on the Kindertransport to England. Who grew up in England?

Solomon Souza

Street Artist who is Painting the World, 1993–

During the day, Jerusalem's outdoor market, Machene Yehuda, is filled with vendors hawking delicacies from hummus to watermelon. At night, when the shopkeepers pull down the metal shutters on their stalls, the market becomes an outdoor modern art gallery. Solomon, an Israeli street artist from Hackney, London, painted most of the 200 murals himself with cans of spray paint.

Solomon's murals show people who he finds inspiring, interesting, or influential—like Golda Meir, Steven Spielberg and several important Arab leaders. Solomon has also painted biblical figures and ordinary Israelis, including several of the shop owners. In the beginning, many shopkeepers asked for murals of their favorite Orthodox rabbis. Solomon obliged until his friends began asking, "Where are the women?" Now he is broader in his choices. Solomon worked on a shoestring budget. "I will forever love the freedom of street painting, the separation of business and creativity, painting just to paint, to influence, shock, and awe. It's an adventure. Something you can never experience while cooped up in a studio," he says.

Today Solomon is a street artist with a global reputation. The Chelsea Football Club in London commissioned him to paint murals of Jewish soccer players killed by the Nazis. His grandfather's town in India invited him to come and paint 20 murals depicting important people from the community. He even designed Torah covers for the Igbo Jewish community of Nigeria.

Solomon's background is diverse. His grandmother was a Jewish actress and his grandfather was a famous modern artist from India. "I am a big mix of a human, a mutt you could say, with roots from India to Israel. . . . I'm able to see the beauty of the world and its differences," says Solomon.

Solomon's earliest memories take place in his mother's art studio in London. "My mother raised me covered in paint, quite literally!" says Solomon. "My youth was filled with creativity, which my mother nurtured and encouraged." Nowadays, Solomon lives in Israel with his wife and strives to pass along creativity to his own young son.

Solomon dreams of forming a *"tzava shel tzeva,"* an army of spray artists, to create more street art in Israel. He believes in the power of art to create community and change. Solomon says "Art is, at its core, self-expression. . . . It's a burst of desire, a need to create and communicate."

Solomon Souza is a self-taught artist.
Who else was self-taught in their craft?

Mel Blanc

The Man of a Thousand Voices, 1908–1989

Bugs Bunny, Woody Woodpecker, Daffy Duck, Porky Pig, Tweety Bird, and the Road Runner. What do they have in common? One man—Mel Blanc—was the voice for all of them. Born in San Francisco and raised in Portland, Oregon, Mel voiced 400 characters and 3,000 cartoons over his career, earning him the nickname "the man of one thousand voices."

Back in high school, however, Mel was known not as a success but as a troublemaker. He skipped class to go to the movies and interrupted his teachers with impersonations. One teacher, Mrs. Washburn, said, "You'll never amount to anything, you're just like your name—a blank." In response, Mel changed the spelling of his name from "Blank" to "Blanc."

While Mel may not have listened to his teachers, he obsessively studied sounds and voices. He said, "I used to look at animals and wonder, how would that kitten sound if it could talk. I'd tighten up my throat and make a very small voice, not realizing I was rehearsing." He was particularly fascinated by his immigrant neighbors' accents. One of his first character voices was based on a Yiddish-speaking couple who ran a nearby shop.

In 1933, Mel married Estelle Rosenbaum and, together, they did a daily radio program. Since the sponsors couldn't afford additional actors, Mel used his voice to create multiple characters at once. He realized he had a unique talent for switching between voices. Soon, Mel was recruited to voice characters for movies and cartoons. When asked to audition for Porky Pig, Mel joked, "You want me to be the voice of a pig? That's some job for a nice Jewish boy." Mel signed an exclusive contract with Warner Brothers to voice every major character in their studio. When that contract expired, Mel worked for other Hollywood studios.

In 1961, Mel was in a horrific car crash on Sunset Boulevard in Los Angeles. For two weeks, Mel was unresponsive in a coma. To jar Mel back to consciousness, his doctors tried in desperation to talk to him as Bugs Bunny. The doctor said, "Bugs, can you hear me?" Mel amazingly responded in character, "Yeah, what's up Doc?"

Thankfully, Mel lived another 28 years, bringing his voice to many more cartoons and movies.

Following his death in 1989, Mel's family inscribed a Jewish star and these words from Loony Tunes on his gravestone—"THAT'S ALL FOLKS."

Shalom Folks!

My Hero

Do you know a hero? Add them to the book!

Hero's Name:

What makes them heroic?

What do you know about their life story?

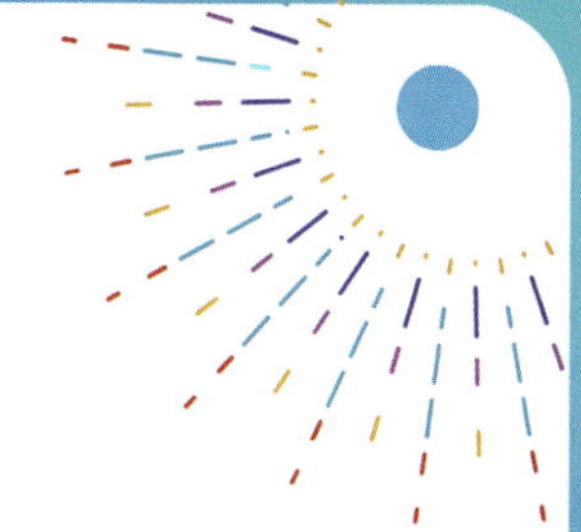

Draw their portrait or
attach a photograph.

About the Authors

Kerry Olitzky

Kerry grew up in the sunny isles of Florida. Although he loved the water, beaches, and wildlife, Kerry didn't feel comfortable in his hometown. He went to a high school whose flag was the Confederate flag, whose school anthem was the Confederate song *Dixie*, and whose school mascot was the Rebels. People of color were not permitted to attend the school, and there was only one other Jewish kid in his graduating class of 1,000. Kerry graduated high school early at 16, then started college in Israel. There he felt included. When he came back to the United States, he finished college and went to Hebrew Union College-Jewish Institute of Religion (HUC-JIR) to study to become a rabbi.

He wrote poetry in college and started writing textbooks while he was in rabbinical school. Kerry loved sharing Jewish texts and making them accessible and meaningful to everybody. After rabbinical school, Kerry led a congregation in Connecticut, then returned to HUC-JIR as a professor.

Kerry never forgot how it felt to be an outsider. He knew some people felt like outsiders in the Jewish community. Kerry wanted everybody to feel comfortable and welcome in the community that he loved. Kerry led an organization called Big Tent Judaism that helped people create warm, welcoming, inclusive Jewish communities.

All the while, he kept writing until he had written nearly 100 books and hundreds of articles. Kerry and his wife Sheryl raised two boys, Avi and Jesse. Both became rabbis themselves! When blessed with grandchildren, he started to write books for them—and for all children.

Deborah Bodin Cohen

By third grade, Debbie still could not read well. At her elementary school in Columbia, Maryland, she was placed in the lowest reading class. This made Debbie wonder whether she was smart. A kind teacher named Mrs. Levy began tutoring Debbie. Mrs. Levy worked in her own classroom with a big wall of books, organized from easiest to hardest.

Debbie and Mrs. Levy started with the easiest book on the wall, but Debbie found it very hard. She could not remember the sounds the vowels made. Then slowly, the letters started to make sense. The books got more challenging, but Debbie found reading easier. At the end of the school year, Mrs. Levy told Debbie that they no longer needed to work together. Debbie didn't want to say good-bye but understood other children needed Mrs. Levy's help. Besides, she had read nearly all the books in Mrs. Levy's classroom.

Debbie studied literature at the University of Michigan. After college, she became a rabbi so she could study the books of the Jewish people. She began writing her own books for children. Debbie has published a dozen books for children and teens. Some of her books have won awards, like a National Jewish Book Award. She even opened her own bookstore for kids. Some letters can still confuse Debbie today, especially if they are spoken rather than written down. But mostly, Debbie has learned to compensate for her learning disability.

These days, Debbie lives in Rockville, Maryland, with her husband David and their children Arianna, Jesse, and Ezra, in a house with a lot of books.

In Gratitude

We are extremely grateful to the nearly 250 people and organizations who believed in Heroes with Chutzpah from the beginning and supported our Kickstarter Campaign. This book would not have been possible without your generous support.

Superheroes

Machon Micah
Representative Alma Hernandez
The Shankman/Namath Family

Heroes

Rabbi Vicki L. Axe
Rabbi Philip Bazeley
Carol & Larry Bodin
The Buber Family
Rabbi Joshua Caruso
Stuart Chaplin
Rabbi Paul Cohen
Cantor Claire Franco
Pamela Garnick
Rabbi David Gelfand
Rabbi Matthew Gewirtz
Shawn and Elisa Gozarkhah
Rabbi Micah Greenstein
Congregation Har HaShem, Boulder, CO
Representative Daniel Hernandez AZ-02
Kimowitz Family
Rabbi Beth H Klafter
Rabbi Marc Kline
Kim, Bruce & Kat Konefsky
Kulanu at Temple Isaiah, Fulton, MD
Ruth Levi
Rabbi Emily Losben-Ostrov and Family
Rabbi Paula Mack Drill & Rabbi Craig Scheff
Carol & David Mersky
Rabbi Ellie Miller
Rabbi Philip Weintraub

Supporters

Steven Altchuler
Anat
Lisa Akselrad
Paul Andinach
David Anshen
Kit Todd-Leo Baker
Tom Ballingall
The Band Family
Pamela Barroway
David Batson
Rachel N. Baum
Rabbi Peter Berg
Isaac Berger
Rabbi Leah Rachel Berkowitz
Cantor Julie Berlin
Melanie Sherry Berman
Sue Bertrand
Marc N. Blattner
Todd Blue
Kim Bodin & Family
Shawna Bodine
The Braskat Arellanes Family
Rabbi Deborah K. Bravo
Rhea Weinberg Brekke
Gayle Brill Mittler
Briskin Elementary School
Sharon Frant Brooks
Rabbi Faith Cantor
The Chafetz Family
Natasha Chisdes
Esmond Choueke
CJAM
Mayda & Alan Clarke
Marc Cohen
Jonathan Cohn
Lisa D'Alonzo
Yona Diamond Dansky
Rabbi Faith Joy Dantowitz
Keren, Shay & Niv Dinur
Erika Dreifus
Pamela Ehrenberg
Toby & Gary Ehrlich
Miriam Eichler
Lucy Carone Elliott
Emmett
Ruthanna Emrys
Jamie Epstein
Robert A. Epstein
Judy Fasman
Lorelei Feldman
Abbi Fiebert
Lindsay Folkerth
Ambassador Meryl Frank
Bonnie & Sheldon Freidenreich
The Freilich Family
Meira Fried
Faith Friedman
Rabbi Neal Gold
The Gonzalez Family
Cathy Green
Susan Green
Rabbi Michael B. & Cindy Greenbaum
Abra Greenspan
Judye Groner
Scott Gurvey
Ed & Bonnie Guttenplan
R.J.H.
Rabbi Richard Hammerman
Rabbi Patti Haskell
The Haynes Family
Aaren Heller
Cantor George & Ricki Henschel
Kate & Ailsa Hermann-Wu
Herzlin Family

Rabbi Joui Hessel
Highland Park Conservative Temple -
Congregation Anshe Emeth
Mark Hirschman
Yael Horowitz
Sharon Hotchkiss
Rabbi Ron Isaacs
Naomi H.J.
Gail Silverstein Jablonski
Robin Jacobson
Misty Jandron
Joy Jones
Dave Joseph (for my 3 daughters)
Rabbi Mark Kaiserman
Kalanit
Alan & Arline Kane
Rabbi Ken Kanter
Rabbi Larry & Rhonda Karol
Mitch Kavalsky
The Kaye-Imlers
Kazmar Family
Zoltan Kemeny
Kirschen Kids
Mira & Milo Krain
Abbe & Edward Krissman
George & Evelyn Lander
The Laufer Family
The Lee family
Jacen Leonard
Bari & Joe Levin
Lewis Family
Marty Linsky
The Little Family
Glen Livesay
A.D. Lobel

Chris and Michal Lockery
Roger Lourie
Rabbi Nicole Luna
Alex M.
Mahler-Gamson Family,
Love for Ari & Brantley
Megan Marsden
Racheal Mastel
Elizabeth R. McClellan
Annika McPeek
Theresa Mecklenborg
Laura Meckler
The Meisegeier Family
Rabbi Amy L. Memis-Foler
Rachel Mersky Woda
Rabbi Michael Greenbaum
Dorit Miles
Michael Wedman & Scott Miller
Debbie & David Miner
Jill Cogan Moghadam
Rabbi Rob Morais
Rabbi Fred Natkin
Ruth Newman z"l
Josh Niesse
Daniel Notowitz
Yevgeniya Nusinovich &
Aaron Ucko
Tia O'Brien
Hazzan Henrique &
Rabbi Janet Ozur Bass
Mandy Pavuk
Professor Abraham J. Peck
Rabbi Wendy Pein
Abigail Pogrebin
Dr. Marilyn Rabinowitz & Family

Rotem Raviv
Reines/Bornstein Family
Rabbi Sara & Ezra Rich
Brian, Sarah, Gabriel, & Charlie Rohr
Lisa & Howard Rosen
The Rosen Family
Rob Rosenberg
Sandra Rosenblatt
The Ross-Lukoff Family:
Jenni, Ben, Ivy, & Lev
Jonathan Roth
Jane Rothstein
David S.
Angelina Salazar-Frank
Susan & Rabbi Neil Sandler
Rabbi Jeffrey Schein
Alyssa Schneyman
The Schoppiks
The Schulman Family
Dr. Matthew L. Schwartz
Rabbi Amy Schwartzman
The Shaiman Family
The Reverends Glenna T. Shepherd &
Marie M. Fortune
Harli Shira
Cantor Yvonne Shore
Elise "Warriorjudge" Simon
Alexander Sims
The Sinton-Remes Family
Rabbi Andrew Sklarz
Slade
Marie Slayton
SLR, for Caleb & Eli
Emilie Smarr
Frank, Morgan & Adriel Smith

Sheila & Ken Sonnenschein
Lynne Sorkin
Alan H. Spiro
In honor of Noam & Ezra Weiner Duran
from Audrey Beth Stein
Craig Taubman
Phil & Amy Taylor
Tasha Turner
Sarena Ulibarri
Phil & Sandy Umansky
Tiffany Updegrove
Rabbi David Z. Vaisberg
The Vaughan-Swartz Family
The Vincent Family
Shelby Voeltz
Noah Weil
Rabbi Jennifer Weiner
Lori R. Weintrob (Wagner College)
Cantor Mike Weis & Family
Kim Werker
Eliana, Alissa & Lielle Whiteman
Louise Whiteman
Brent G. Wilson
Rabbi Paula Jayne Winnig
Keren Witkin
Kathryn Wolf
Rabbi Stephanie Wolfe
Rabbi Julie Wolkoff
Gail Yarosh
Mindel Zelda
Jamie Zelermyer
Tom, Heidi & Sarah Zellman

Photo and Art Credits

Author Deborah Bodin Cohen created the portraits in this book by using photographs and a variety of digital tools, including photo editing and graphic software.

Images not listed in the photo credits are public domain, came from Canva, or were drawn using Procreate.

The authors thank the following for permission to use their photographs:

Paula Abdul – Shutterstock/DFree

Yossi Abramowitz – Shutterstock

Bella Abzug – *Life* Magazine cover: Alamy/Patti McConville; Pins: Creative Commons/Flickr/Mpls55408

Red Auerbach – In Tux: City of Boston Archives, Boston, Creative Commons Attribution 2.0; On bench with Boston Celtics center Bill Russell: *The Sporting News* Archives, Author Jack O'Connell, public domain; Norm Drucker ejecting Boston Celtic coach Red Auerbach from a game in 1959: NEA public domain; Team picture: Unknown photographer, public domain; In arena: Steve Lipofsky at basketballphoto.com. Creative Commons Attribution-Share Alike 3.0

Yityish Titi Aynaw – Photo: Israeli Embassy

David Ben-Gurion – Alamy/DPA Picture Alliance

Moe Berg – Wikimedia Commons/public domain: 1933 Goudey baseball card of Morris "Moe" Berg of the Washington Senators #158

Mayim Bialik – Shutterstock/Joe Seer

Sue Bird – Shutterstock/Dmitry Argunov

Judy Blume – Alamy/Reuters. Photographer: Lucy Nicholson

Albert Bourla – Alamy/Reuters. Photographer: John Thys

Angela Buchdahl – Photo courtesy of Jewish Women's Archives, taken by Angela Jimenez in 2013

Leonard Cohen – Leonard Cohen Photo: Alamy. Painting of King David: Gerard van Honthorst, King David Playing the Harp, 1622

Stosh Cotler – Photo courtesy of Stosh Cotler

Rachel Cowan – Photo courtesy of the Cowan family

Daveed Diggs – Shutterstock/DFree

Rebecca Dubowe – Photo courtesy of Rebecca Dubowe

Gertrude Elion – Courtesy of the Gertrude B. Elion Foundation

Eytan Fox – Main photo: Eytan Fox at the 2012 Tribeca Film Festival premiere of *Yossi*, David Shankbone, Creative Commons Attribution 3.0. Soldiers in snow: Shutterstock/David Cohen. Man at beach with arms open: Shutterstock/Vitalii Matokha. Man at Dead Sea: Shutterstock/Olesia Bilkei. Tel Aviv with woman: Shutterstock/Emanuele Nocerino. Soldier: Shutterstock/Ryan Rodrick Beiler

Debbie Friedman – Photos courtesy of Susan Shane Linder

Gal Gadot – Shutterstock/DFree

Uzia Galil – Photo of Uzia Galil: Library of Israel, The Aryeh Kalev Archive. Image of Matam: Shutterstock/Galia. Background of Haifa Hills: Shutterstock/Kateryna Mashkevych

Frank Gehry – Portrait photo: Alamy/Abacapress. Building photo: Shutterstock/Nature's Charm

Amit Goffer – Alamy Stock/Reuters

Alma Hernandez – Photo by Gage Skidmore, Creative Commons 3

Anat Hoffman – Courtesy of Flash90/photographer Hadas Parush

Sara Hurwitz – Photo courtesy of Sara Hurwitz

Eddie Jacobson – Photo courtesy of Truman Presidential Library and Museum

Ágnes Keleti – Photos courtesy of the Hungarian Olympic Committee

Edward Kessler – Photo: Foreign & Commonwealth Office in London, Creative Commons 2

Kivie Kaplan – John F. Kennedy

Presidential Library and Museum, Boston
Lynne Landsberg – Lynne Landsberg
Aaron Lansky – Portrait courtesy of Aaron Lansky. Background images, Library of Congress, public domain
Amichai Lau-Lavie – Photos courtesy of Amichai Lau-Lavie
Ralph Lauren – Alamy Stock Photo/Retro Ad Archives
Stan Lee – Shutterstock/Jaguar PS
Annie Leibovitz – Alamy/Interfoto
Joe Levin Jr. – Portrait: Courtesy of Joe Levin Jr. Photo of original SPLC staff: Courtesy of the SPLC
Joseph Lieberman – Photo of man praying: Shutterstock/Poleznova
Deborah Lipstadt – Portrait: Alamy/PA images. Background Photo: Shutterstock/Everett Collection
Idina Menzel – Shutterstock/Lev Radin. Taken at the 2014 Macy's Thanksgiving Day Parade
Harvey Milk – Gay Historical Commission/San Francisco Public Library
Isaac Mizrahi – Adapted from Creative Commons/Rhododendrites
Miguel Najdorf – National Archives of the Netherlands/Creative Commons
Leonard Nimoy – Image of Leonard Nimoy from postage stamp: Shutterstock/spatuletail. Spaceship image from postage stamp: Shutterstock/Olga Popova
Claudia Sheinbaum Pardo – Shutterstock/Octavio Hoyos
Arno Penzias – Alamy/Reuters
Itzhak Perlman – Alamy/United Archives
Natalie Portman – Image of Natalie Portman: Alamy Stock Photo/Lucasfilm Album. Background photo: Shutterstock/Anton Balazh
Sally Priesand – Image of Sally Priesand: Jewish Women's Archives. Image of girl: Shutterstock/Jeka
Yitzchak Rabin – National Library of Israel
Daniel Radcliffe – Shutterstock/Matteo Chinellato
Jamie Raskin – Alamy/Reuters
Aly Raisman – Shutterstock/Salty View
Moshe Safdie – Photo of Moshe Safdie taken by Michal Ronnen Safdie, Creative Commons Attribution-Share Alike 4.0. Photos of design projects in background from Creative Commons and Wikimedia Commons
Jonas Salk – Alamy/Pictorial Press Ltd
Sheryl Sandberg – Alamy/DPA Picture Alliance
Bernie Sanders – Shutterstock/Rich Koele
David Saperstein – Alamy/DPA Picture Alliance
Maurice Sendak – Portrait: Courtesy of Archives & Special Collections, UConn Library. Photographer: Jo Lincoln. Wild Thing: Shutterstock/from postage stamp
Avital Sharansky – Alamy/David Parker
Danny Siegel – Photos courtesy of Danny Siegel
Sarah Silverman – Main photo: Shutterstock/Featureflash Photo Agency. Secondary photo: Shutterstock/S. Bukley
Becky Silverstein – Photo courtesy of Becky Silverstein
Gershom Sizomu – Photo courtesy of Gershom Sizomu
Solomon Souza – Photos by Deborah Bodin Cohen
Steven Spielberg – Shutterstock/DFree
Mark Spitz – Alamy/Patti McConville
Abby Stein – Photo courtesy of Abby Stein
Gloria Steinem – Alamy/American Photo Archive
Helen Suzman – Photo courtesy of the Suzman family/appeared on postage stamp. Photo behind: Shutterstock/spatuletail
Jacobo Timerman – Bernard Gotfryd photograph collection (Library of Congress)
Michael Twitty – Photo courtesy of Michael Twitty. Photographer: Noah Fecks
Simone Veil – Portrait: Alamy/Pascal Baril. Photo of Simone Veil in background: National Archives of the Netherlands. Street sign: Creative Commons Attribution-Share Alike 4.0 International; contributor: Chabe01
Naomi Wadler – Reuters/Alamy Stock Photo
Randi Weingarten – Alamy/DPA Picture Alliance
Elie Wiesel – Shutterstock/Lev Radin
Volodymyr Zelenskyy – Shutterstock/Dmytro Larin

Heroes Index

Sources for all quotations can be found at www.HeroesWithChutzpah.com.

Who's Who

Actors and Entertainers: Paula Abdul (p. 150), Yityish "Titi" Aynaw (p. 80), Mayim Bialik (p. 92), Mel Blanc (p. 200), Eytan Fox (p. 140), Gal Gadot (p. 78), Leonard Nimoy (p. 90), Natalie Portman (p. 98), Daniel Radcliffe (p. 182), Sarah Silverman (p. 2), Anna Sokolow (p. 40), Steven Spielberg (p. 84), Barbara Walters (p. 124).

Athletics and Competitions: Red Auerbach (p. 170), Moe Berg (p. 100), Sue Bird (p. 172), Ágnes Keleti (p. 58), Sandy Koufax (p. 102), Emerich "Imi" Lichtenfeld (p. 142), Miguel Najdorf (p. 156), Aly Raisman (p. 148), Mark Spitz (p. 56), Yosef Yekutieli (p. 60).

Artists and Architects: Frank Gehry (p. 120), Frida Kahlo (p. 32), Annie Leibovitz (p. 66), Moshe Safdie (p. 118), Solomon Souza (p. 198).

Entrepreneurs and Business Leaders: Yossi Abramowitz (p. 4), Jennie Grossinger (p. 168), Eddie Jacobson (p. 164), Ralph Lauren (p. 64), Isaac Mizrahi (p. 166), Sheryl Sandberg (p. 146).

Government

United States: Bella Savitzky Abzug (p. 42), Douglas Emhoff (p. 62), Ruth Bader Ginsberg (p. 110), Alma Hernandez (p. 186), Elena Kagan (p. 46), Joseph Lieberman (p. 108), Harvey Milk (p. 138), Jamie Raskin (p. 44), Bernie Sanders (p. 106), Janet Yellen (p. 174).

Israel: David Ben-Gurion (p. 158), Yitzhak Rabin (p. 160).

Other Countries: Claudia Sheinbaum Pardo (p. 72), Helen Suzman (p. 50), Simone Veil (p. 114), Volodymyr Zelenskyy (p. 68).

Interfaith Relations: Rachel Cowan (p. 134), Edward Kessler (p. 162).

Jewish Thought Leaders: Angela Warnick Buchdahl (p. 130), Rebecca Dubowe (p. 184), Sara Hurwitz (p. 48), Regina Jonas (p. 12), Aaron Lansky (p. 88), Amichai Lau-Lavie (p. 178), Sally Priesand (p. 10), Becky Silverstein (p. 192), Gershom Sizomu (p. 52), Abby Stein (p. 180).

Musicians: Leonard Cohen (p. 26), Daveed Diggs (p. 152), Bob Dylan (p. 22), Debbie Friedman (p. 24), Idina Menzel (p. 96), Itzhak Perlman (p. 86).

Science and Technology: Simcha Blass (p. 74), Albert Bourla (p. 28), Judith Love Cohen (p. 194), Gertrude "Trudy" Elion (p. 8), Uzia Galil (p. 144), Amit Goffer (p. 122), Hedy Lamarr (p. 76), Arno Penzias (p. 196), Judith Resnick (p. 38), Jonas Salk (p. 30).

Social Justice: Stosh Cotler (p. 128), Andrew Goodman (p. 136), Anat Hoffman (p. 54), Kivie Kaplan (p. 20), Lynne Landsberg (p. 18), Joe Levin Jr. (p. 112), Deborah Lipstadt (p. 14), David Saperstein (p. 16), Avital Sharansky (p. 70), Danny Siegel (p. 176), Gloria Steinem (p. 126), Jacobo Timerman (p. 155), Naomi Wadler (p. 82), Randi Weingarten (p. 104), Simon Wiesenthal (p. 116).

Writers: Judy Blume (p. 94), Ann Landers (p. 190), Stan Lee (p. 36), Moacyr Scliar (p. 188), Maurice Sendak (p. 34), Michael Twitty (p. 132), Abigail Van Buren (p. 190), Elie Wiesel (p. 6).

Also Available from Ben Yehuda Press

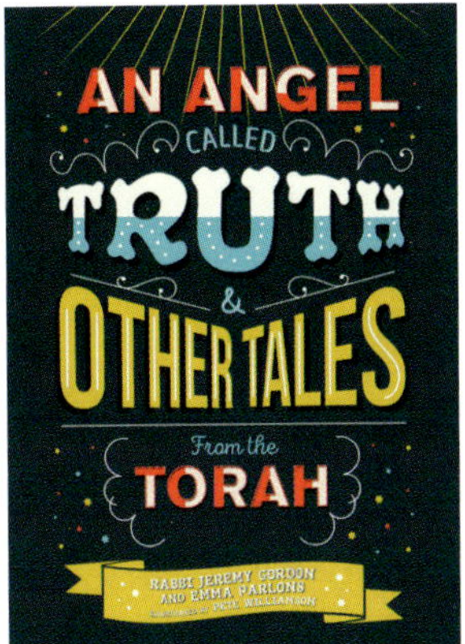

An Angel Called Truth and Other Tales from the Torah
by Rabbi Jeremy Gordon and Emma Parlons

Short, engaging stories related to the weekly Torah portion written for kids 10 to 13. These new tales are matched with breathtaking artwork by Pete Williamson. A vibrant cast of characters, primarily children—though with an occasional angel, as in the title story—bring a new twist to each week's Torah portion and to each Jewish holiday.

Each story also includes discussion questions to connect the "back then" of the stories to the "right now" lives of today's kids, making ***An Angel Called Truth*** the perfect companion for Shabbat table conversations or Hebrew school discussions.

"A delightful, accessible, engaging introduction to midrash for kids. I know it'll be in heavy rotation in my home; I imagine yours, too." —Rabbi Danya Ruttenberg, author of *On Repentance and Repair* and *Nurture the Wow*

Eyn Fish Tsvey Fish Royter Fish Bloyer Fish
by Dr. Seuss, translated by Sholem Berger

"Eyn fish/Tsvey fish/Royter fish/Bloyer fish"

Thus begins the classic children's book of Dr. Seuss's imaginative menagerie, now translated into Yiddish, the language that brought the world gefilte fish.

Eyn Fish, Tzvey Fish features the illustrations of Dr. Seuss and rhyming *mamaloshen* that captures the words, rhyme scheme, and spirit of the original. Its text is written in both *alef-bais* and transliteration, and there's an alphabet chart to help those not yet proficient in Yiddish.

You Be You (Yiddish Edition)
The Kid's Guide to Gender, Sexuality, and Family
by Jonathan Branfman
translated into contemporary Hassidic Yiddish by Lili Rosen

This is an illustrated Yiddish children's book for ages 7-11 that makes gender identity, sexual orientation and family diversity easy to explain to children.

Throughout the book kids learn that there are many kinds of people in the world and that diversity is something to be celebrated. It covers gender, romantic orientation, discrimination, intersectionality, privilege, and how to stand up for what's right. With charming illustrations, clear explanations, and short sections that can be dipped in and out of, this book helps children think about how to create a kinder, more tolerant world.

Sarah Silverman's brother-in-law is **Yossi Abramowitz** whose professor wa
work because of her gender like **Sally Priesand**, who everybody thought w
the same actress, in a different movie, as **Deborah Lipstadt**, a United St
building named for **Kivie Kaplan** who participated in the 1963 March on
Debbie Friedman who was influenced by **Leonard Cohen** who lived in Gr
Salk who created a vaccine for polio, a disease that unfortunately impair
who worked with Sesame Street as did **Stan Lee** who created the Captai
considered studying at The Juilliard School where one of the professors was
like **Jamie Raskin** who was an editor of the Harvard Law Review like **Elen**
grew up in South Africa like **Helen Suzman** who served in an African parli
Anat Hoffman who won medals in swimming at the Maccabiah Games as
Keleti who first came to Israel because of the Maccabiah Games, founde
his wife's inauguration designed by **Ralph Lauren** who has been photogr
Russian pressure as did **Avital Sharansky** who never planned on going int
environment like **Simcha Blass** who liked to tinker and invent as did **Hedy**
Yityish "Titi" Aynaw who was born in Ethiopia as was **Naomi Walder** who s
who directed Schindler's List which features music played by **Itzhak Perl**
Aaron Lansky, which produced a documentary about **Leonard Nimoy** wh
books by **Judy Blume** who graduated from New York University like **Idina**
six languages, which is four less than **Moe Berg** who played for the Dodge
Weingarten who campaigned for **Bernie Sanders**, a senator who served f
Supreme Court Justice **Ruth Bader Ginsburg** who argued a case in front
Simone Veil who survived the Holocaust as did **Simon Wiesenthal** who ori
and neither did **Frank Gehry** who is inspired by nature and biological str
and neither did **Barbara Walters** who interviewed **Gloria Steinem** who is
Angela Warnick Buchdahl who delights in merging her different identities
a Freedom Rider like **Andrew Goodman** who stood up for his values despite
Eytan Fox who incorporates Krav Maga into his movies, a martial arts sys
Holocaust as did **Uzia Galil** who was a pioneer in establishing high-tech inc
like **Aly Raisman** who has appeared on Dancing with the Stars as has **Paul**
harassment as did **Jacobo Timerman** who escaped antisemitism in Europ
Europe as did **David Ben-Gurion** who served as Israel's prime minister as di
considers trusting relationships vital as did **Eddie Jacobson** who sold cloth
Grossinger who believed in racial integration as did **Red Auerbach** who
like **Janet Yellen** who watched her father's patients struggle to afford medi
Seminary of America like **Amichai Lau-Lavie** who was born into a rabbin
Daniel Radcliffe who has learned to compensate for a disability as has **R**
who blends her Latin American and Jewish heritages like **Moacyr Scliar** w
who were twins as is **Becky Silverstein** who studied engineering like **Judith**
Nazi Germany on the Kindertransport to England, the home country of **S**